Lost Desserts

GAIL MONAGHAN

Lost Desserts

DELICIOUS INDULGENCES OF THE PAST

Recipes from Legendary Restaurants and Famous Chefs

Photographs by

ERIC BOMAN

Foreword by

GEORGE LANG

RIZZOLI
NEW YORK

For Iva

Contents

FROZEN DESSERTS

Foreword

BY GEORGE LANG

O n one of my birthdays, after an all-night party, my wife Jennifer arranged eighty birthday cakes, each made by another pastry chef around the world. Sometime around midnight I had a strange encounter with an elderly gentleman, who was looking at me with his mesmerizing eyes, surprised that I had sampled bites of at least three dozen of the birthday cakes. Fortunately, I remembered Mark Twain's line and told him, "The secret is to eat what you like and let the food fight it out inside."

What this mysterious person did not know was that during the past couple of decades, I had become a dessert addict, tasting and, mostly, enjoying their flavors.

What we need today is a book that gives precise and stylish instructions for making sweets our ancestors made and enjoyed. I am happy to say that Gail Monaghan's volume, *Lost Desserts*, is a brilliant collection. She brings to us practical and contemporary versions of great sweets of yesterday made with today's ingredients and techniques.

Reading her book reminded me that I learned quite a bit about this sweet subject in Hungary, the country of my birth, where some of the experts claim that the Aztecs shamelessly stole the secret of making chocolate from a Budapest housewife. Even though Hungarian housewives and pastry chefs make memorable desserts, I have a bit of a problem with this Danubian statement.

A few weeks ago, five friends of ours from the world of restaurants were enjoying our coffee when one of the guests asked us to mention desserts that are truly close to us. I have to admit that dessert names were thrown around without rules to follow, but I recall a few of the names that each of us declared during this session. Here is a list: Charlotte Russe, Chocolate Angel Torte, Dobos Torte, Escoffier's Peach Melba, and Schrafft's Coffee Milkshake.

The most engaging power of an author or a cook is to make new things familiar and—surprise—familiar things new. When James Beard was asked, "What is the best part of a dessert?" he said, "It is the anticipation." You might start anticipating by reading this great book of Gail Monaghan's recipes.

And now I think I should mention another of my dear late friend James Beard's remarks: "A gourmet who thinks of calories is like a tart who looks at her watch." Sociology even today is an inexact science, but it is safe to say that the first step is to love the past. It is a pleasure to tell you that this book is warm, sweet, and comforting, just like stories your nanny would have told you.

Not wanting to be expelled from the Hungarian Academy of Sciences, I should tell you about Emperor Claudius, who, according to a Hungarian historian, once visited the Roman Senate and asked the members, "What do you think? Is it possible to live without smoked bacon?" Their answer was, "It is possible, but in a sad state." If I was a member of the U.S. Senate and the same questions were asked of me regarding Gail Monaghan's *Lost Desserts*, my unhesitating answer would follow the Roman senators' observation.

There is an old-fashioned timepiece called the skeleton clock whose face has been removed to display its inner workings. Monaghan simplifies re-creating the dessert recipes by removing the dizzying array of irrelevant components, and, most importantly, updating them for today's home cooks.

Finally, serious advice from me: Some cookbooks are for reading, some for reference, and others—very few—can be cherished and kept right in the kitchen. I hope Gail Monaghan's *Lost Desserts* will have a special place in yours.

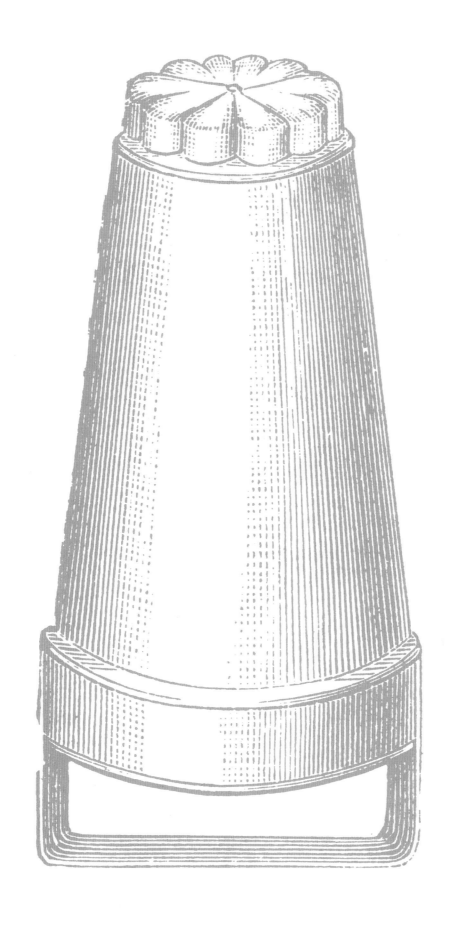

Introduction

This book has been long in the making. When I think back, it all began with my childhood love of heavily iced birthday cake à la mode. First there was a big flat vanilla sheetcake from Ralph's, our local supermarket chain. It was covered with white frosting and, most important, lots of pink roses. Next came one from a bakery in the Los Angeles Farmers Market famous for cakes heavily iced in the shop's version of "marshmallow fluff." What was really special about these cakes were the scenes decorating them—overblown, Botero-like clowns, flowers, Disney figures, whatever you wanted—brightly colored and enormous, often six to eight inches high. When I turned twelve and saw myself as a young lady, I favored the exact opposite, an elegant and minimalist cake—two simple genoise layers filled and iced with coffee buttercream, then garnished with a fine sprinkling of pulverized almonds—from Bailey's, our local European-style bakery. Adorned with extra-slender special birthday candles my mother discovered somewhere, this remained my birthday cake of choice until I left for college.

My early love of desserts was nurtured by sugar-loving relatives who endlessly indulged my sweet tooth. Grandma Rose baked me angel and chiffon pies in every conceivable flavor and color of the rainbow; several versions of cheesecake; a perfect pineapple upside-down cake; and blintzes smothered in sour cream and jam. Aunt Iva was the first person I knew to have an electric ice-cream maker, and she experimented with more ice-cream flavors than I knew existed. Hers was also my first Dobos Torte, the recipe meticulously followed from a 1950 *Gourmet Cookbook*. My mother, always trying to avoid dessert but then eventually succumbing, made me Lemon Chiffon Pie, her famous Trifle Pudding in the heavy glass bowl handed down from her great aunt, and Baked Alaska, using lemon custard ice cream purchased from the recently opened Baskin Robbins. She would also bring home special treats from Bailey's; my favorite was a divine cookie sandwiching vanilla buttercream between two almond macaroons, then dipped in chocolate and walnut-studded.

The Los Angeles of my childhood was a dessert-lover's paradise. Beverly Hills was the home of the first Baskin Robbins with its 31 flavors of ice cream (my favorite back then was jamocha almond fudge). Less than a mile from my doorstep, Blum's introduced me to Coffee Crunch Cake and Coffiesta Sundaes, and Pupi's, on Sunset Boulevard, had the best chocolate cake in town.

Also right there on Sunset was the surprisingly-chic-for-the-era Wil Wright's ice-cream parlor serving the first espresso ice cream I ever tasted and probaby the first in America (always accompanied by the signature mini macaroon slipped into a little wax paper case).

These deliciously formative childhood memories never left me, and just a few years ago I found myself baking a Blum's Coffee Crunch Cake for Lora Zarubin's birthday dinner. Lora works at *House and Garden*, as did several other dinner guests. Everyone loved the cake and soon we were discussing lost Los Angeles desserts in general. By the end of the evening, a "Lost Desserts" story—based on recollections from my California childhood—was in the works.

With difficulty I narrowed my selection of favorites to six, five of which are included in this book (Blum's Coffee Crunch Cake, Romanoff's Baked Alaska, Chasen's Banana Shortcake, The Brown Derby's Orange Chiffon Cake, and Scandia's Princess Cake). Later, having decided to expand the article into a book, I spoke with friends and friends of friends, collecting their family recipes, anecdotes, and culinary secrets. I include some of this heirloom material here; but, in the end, decided to focus primarily on restaurant recipes that are "lost" specifically because the restaurants, or the chefs, no longer exist. However, I did end up with a few non-restaurant desserts, either because they were too delicious and/or unusual to ignore—Seidel Torte, Zausner's Crème Fraîche Cheesecake, Friars' Ears, and Fané—or because such desserts as Bavarians, charlottes, fools, jellies, and Mont Blanc were once classics and are too fabulous to be relegated to oblivion.

Like most books, this one is a personal statement. Everyone with whom I discussed the project had different favorites, different opinions. For example, while many felt that île flottante (floating island) was an obligatory inclusion, in the end it just did not seem lost enough to me. Instead I chose Helen Corbitt's Caramel Soufflé (a more interesting variation on the French dessert and identical to the Portuguese Molotov Pudding), in which the traditional vanilla-flavored meringue is replaced by a caramel-flavored one. Oeufs à la neige (eggs in snow) fell into that same category of not lost enough. I deliberated over syllabubs (Elizabeth David has excellent recipes in her *Syllabubs and Fruit Fools*), but ultimately I don't find them that tasty, and I am prejudiced against drinking my dessert. Barbara Kafka pushed for a chiffon pie, but unique though they are, again for me they do not qualify as sufficiently lost. Pain perdu was a contender. (How could I not include something whose name actually implied "lostness"?) But even though it is not seen on dessert menus anymore, French toast as a breakfast or brunch food is still with us. I omitted Indian pudding from my original list for a completely different reason; try as I might, I could not make one that I deemed edible. An ex-pastry chef from a top-notch New York restaurant once told me that every cook has something he or she cannot make. This particular woman could not make meringue. I think my Achilles' heel must be Indian pudding.

If this book were twice as long, a Southern cake—such as Lady Baltimore or Emma Lane's prize cake—would have made its appearance, as well as stack cakes, and chess and grasshopper pies, also from the American South. There would have been another old English standby or two such as trifle and tipsy puddings, very similar to each other and assembled from trifles (a bit of this and a bit of that)—almonds, jam, and whipped cream layered between Madeira- or brandy-soaked (the tipsy-causing agent) sponge layers and served in cut-glass bowls. Bakewell and treacle tarts, the first a jam, almond, and egg creation baked in a pastry shell; the second quite a bit like a pecan pie but minus the pecans—too sweet for some, its main ingredient being Lyle's golden syrup. A Proustian favorite, Nesselrode pudding would also have its spot. Not really a pudding but a chestnut-flavored frozen bombe made with dried and candied fruits and maraschino liqueur, the most famous of many dishes named after Count Nesselrode, a prominent nineteenth-century Russian diplomat. Another French dessert worthy of resurrection, subtly sublime when made properly, is blancmange, a gelatin and milk or cream mixture delicately flavored with almond, chilled, and then unmolded . . . there are so many wonderful desserts that have been lost or at least misplaced with the passage of time.

My editor encouraged me to update the desserts, to make them more in sync with a modern palate. I loved the license this gave me to play with the recipes, but I did try to stay true to the original concepts and flavors. (The one exception to this was my adding ginger to the more tradi-tional caramelized rice pudding. I just couldn't resist.) I've adapted the recipes found here from restaurant and other cookbooks, old newspaper and magazine articles, and from those passed on to me by friends and relatives. A few, tempered I'm sure by tricks of memory and the passage of time, derive solely from wonderfully delicious recollections of restaurant meals eaten long ago.

My favorite quote in all cookingdom is in the preface to Brillat-Savarin's 1956 *Real French Cooking*, where Maurice Saillant-Curnonsky is quoted as saying, " . . . you do not invent a new dish by pouring fish soup over a sirloin nor yet by smothering a jugged hare in peppermint . . . a superfine dish is the master achievement of many generations." I have always preferred tried-and-true dessert-trolley fare, comprised of fairly basic ingredients, to the currently more popular, some-times too-precious plated dessert. I'll take an old-fashioned layer cake, flan, cheesecake, or sticky toffee pudding any day over chocolate that tastes like green tea or a crème anglaise flavored with porcini or basil. So for me, working on this book, surrounded by whipped cream, marzipan, cus-tard, buttercream, meringue, fresh fruit, and spun sugar was a delight. And even better was doing it alongside Carême, Escoffier, Fernand Point, Eduard de Pomiane, Edouard Nignon, Marcel Boulestin, and so many other food greats of the past—Curnonksy, Brillat-Savarin, Elizabeth Pennell, the Vicomte de Mauduit, and more. Reading the recipes, words, biographies, and autobi-ographies of these remarkable people was mesmerizing. And the reminiscences . . . nothing could be more satisfying than joining Joseph Wechsberg, A. J. Liebling, Elizabeth David, M. F. K. Fisher, or Lady Agnes Jekyll as they ended their meals with one glorious dessert after another.

FOOLS, MOUSSES, and CREAMS

Auguste Escoffier's Mont Blanc

Charlotte Russe

Arcadia's Lemon Curd Mousse in Almond Tuile Cups

Gooseberry Fool

Marbled Rose and Raspberry Fool

Salammbos

Sauternes Bavarian Cream

Mont Blanc

This dessert classic was created by legendary chef and restaurateur Auguste Escoffier, whose collaboration with hotelier César Ritz changed the history of fine dining forever. In 1884 Ritz needed a chef at his Grand Hotel in Monte Carlo; Escoffier, who was working at his uncle's hotel in nearby Nice, was hired for the job. This was fortuitous for both men and went on to give the definition of luxury hotel living and dining new meaning. The efforts of this visionary team dramatically advanced the culinary arts in France and, ultimately, worldwide. Ritz had developed an idea of what a *luxe* hotel should be and knew that superb dining was a necessary part of the package; until joining up with Escoffier, however, he was not able to totally realize his dream. Likewise, no one had appreciated Escoffier's talents to the fullest or given him a stage on which to showcase them until he met Ritz. From the start, Ritz got it: In *César Ritz, Host to the World*, Marie Louise Ritz quotes him as saying: "*M. Escoffier est certainement le premier cuisinière du monde, il depasse de beaucoup tous les autres chefs que j'ai rencontré.*" These two men were sticklers for both form and quality. Excellent food had to be accompanied by impeccable service and perfect presentation, and also be accented by a touch of theater—but dramatic only up to a point. When asked by a reporter if he would fall on his own sword (a reference to Vatel, the chef of the Prince de Condé who, in 1671, did just that when the Dover sole had not arrived from across the channel in time for a royal dinner), Escoffier replied, "No, I would have made a mousse of young chicken breasts and covered it with a fish velouté, and nobody would have known the difference."

Ritz and Escoffier were amazing innovators and, above all, worshiped simplicity. They reflected the time in which they lived, when there was a strong movement to reject the pompous and overdone in dress, literature, theater, and the visual arts. Ritz was busy "abolishing senseless ornament and dust-collecting fabric," while Escoffier was substituting a sprinkling of parsley and a few simple vegetables for useless inedible garnishes. He jettisoned the elaborate pedestals and architectural *pièces montées* centerpieces typical of Antonin Carême, as well as the commonly used decorative cockscombs and crayfish impaled on skewers. At the same time he simplified menus and sauces, often repeating Mallarmé's statement that, "food should look like food," rather than like Greek temples or jewelry or "specimens of taxidermy."

In his groundbreaking *Le Guide Culinaire* (1907), Escoffier clearly details his innovative principles, ideas, and recipes, as revolutionary at the time as Carême in his day or *nouvelle cuisine* in the 1960s. Escoffier is as famous for this book, written as a guide for future chefs of large restaurants, as for his brilliant achievements in hotel kitchens. In her book *Great Cooks and Their*

Recipes, Anne Willan gives Escoffier credit for "finally putting an end to the medieval principle of luxurious display. After 500 years, quantity had at last surrendered to quality, and gluttony to gourmandise."

After the Grand in Monte Carlo, the team of Ritz-Escoffier remade Lucerne's Hotel National, London's Savoy, and the Paris Ritz. The rich and famous flocked to these establishments, where they were lavishly indulged. When the wedding of the Duke of Aosta and Princess Helene, the sister of the Duke of Orléans, was held at the Savoy, Escoffier simultaneously served thirty-seven princes, princesses, dukes, and duchesses at one table, while serving their entourages at a different table and in another room fifty members of the Cornish Club, presided over by the Prince of Wales. And all three tables had completely different menus!

What was most revolutionary about the Ritz-Escoffier team was their popularization of restaurant dining. In late-1800s Victorian England, the only women who ate in restaurants were actresses, singers, and members of the *demi-mondaine*; others did not dine out for fear of being taken for mistresses. The charming and persuasive César Ritz convinced these proper ladies to dine in public for the first time, and Escoffier created many of his best dishes with a woman's palate in mind. *Le tout Paris*, and *tout le monde*, showed up in droves, everyone from Sarah Bernhardt, the Prince of Wales, Bismarck, and Lord Chamberlain to the Rothschilds, Morgans, Vanderbilts, Crespis, and the grand dukes of Russia.

In *Larousse Gastronomique*, the Mont Blanc is described as "a cold dessert made of vanilla-flavored chestnut purée, topped with a dome of Chantilly cream and decorated." The complex flavor and somewhat starchy texture of the chestnuts stands out particularly well against the plain but rich simplicity of the cream. However, there are many variations on this theme. Most involve peeling, cooking, and puréeing chestnuts, then mixing the purée with some or all of the following: milk, cream, butter, sugar, vanilla, and sugar syrup. But I find Escoffier's original recipe in his *Ma Cuisine* (1934) the simplest, and best, of all. The chestnuts are cooked and put through a ricer into a ring mold. Then the contents are inverted onto a platter and sprinkled with vanilla sugar. The chestnut taste is stronger this way than if the purée were adulterated by the addition of cream, butter, milk, or sugar. This recipe is very easy—yet another example of Escoffier's genius.

The ring-mold presentation, with a "white mountain" made of an "irregular and jagged mound of sugared and vanilla-flavored whipped cream" in the center, is traditional. Sometimes, however, the chantilly cream is piled in the center of the platter (on a base of meringue, sablé pastry, or a Kirsch-flavored cake or savarin—or not) and surrounded by the riced chestnuts. Sometimes a mountain of riced chestnut purée is completely masked by the whipped cream. And sometimes, especially in French patisseries, the dessert is served in individual portions, usually on meringues.

In *The Escoffier Cookbook* Escoffier gives a variation, Mont Blanc with Strawberries, in which he omits chestnuts altogether. He folds wild strawberries soaked in vanilla syrup into very stiff whipped cream, which he then makes into a mountain. He surrounds this "mountain" with whole strawberries dipped in egg white and sugar, and decorates the surface with "very large and very red halved strawberries." Not so bad for Valentine's Day, if you can find good strawberries in February!

Serves 8 to 10

2 pounds fresh chestnuts
1 vanilla bean, split and scraped
½ teaspoon salt
½ cup granulated sugar
About 1 quart whole milk
About ¼ cup vanilla sugar (see page 191), plus enough
     to dust the mold
2 cups very cold heavy cream
1½ teaspoons vanilla extract

1. Make a deep slit in the flat side of each chestnut. Place the chestnuts in a large pot of boiling water, bring back to a boil, and boil for 5 minutes. Turn off the heat. Remove a few chestnuts at a time, keeping the rest hot, and remove the shell and inner skin.

2. When all the chestnuts are peeled (or they can be tightly wrapped and frozen for a month or more at this point), rinse out the pot and put the peeled chestnuts back in it. To the pot add the vanilla bean and seeds, the salt, and ¼ cup of the granulated sugar; add enough milk to just cover. Cook, partially covered and stirring frequently (especially near the end so the chestnuts do not stick or burn), over medium heat until the chestnuts are very tender, about 20 minutes.

At this point, the milk will probably all be absorbed. If not, place the chestnuts in a strainer and drain. If they seem dry enough, try passing a few through a potato ricer. If they fall vermicelli-like and lightly, and hold their shape, that is good. If they are too wet to hold their shape, put the chestnuts back in the empty pan and stir them over medium heat for a couple of minutes to dry them out, then test again. If they are too dry to go through the ricer, add a couple of tablespoons of milk and try again. You should loosely pack the ricer. If it is too densely packed you will have trouble pushing the chestnuts through. (Note: Even under the best of circumstances, if the chestnuts are dry enough to hold their shape it will take a bit of effort to push them through.)

3. Pass the chestnuts, in batches, through the ricer; the chestnuts will be lighter and fluffier if riced twice. For the second pass, butter a ring mold and dust it with vanilla sugar. Then pass the chestnuts through the ricer in batches again and, moving it around, fill the mold as evenly as possible. Between batches, lightly sprinkle the riced chestnuts with vanilla sugar. Using two forks, gently pick up any riced chestnuts that have fallen outside the mold and place them inside.

4. Turn the filled mold out onto a platter and sprinkle with the remaining vanilla sugar.

5. Whip the cream together with the remaining ¼ cup sugar and the vanilla extract until soft peaks form. Fill the center of the molded chestnuts with lots of the vanilla whipped cream to, as Escoffier says, "approximate the snowy peaks of Mont Blanc." The chestnuts can be riced several hours ahead and the dessert unmolded and covered with a large bowl, but do not top with whipped cream until ready to serve.

Charlotte Russe

Confusion abounds when differentiating between a charlotte and a Charlotte Russe. Although both are prepared in bread, cake, or ladyfinger-lined molds, the original charlotte is a baked fruit dessert served warm, while the Charlotte Russe (which came later) is an unbaked custard set with gelatin.

The Charlotte Russe is thought to have been invented in Second Empire France (1852–70) by Antonin Carême, who probably came across the classic Apple Charlotte a few years earlier while in England working for the prince regent. Carême first called his dessert *charlotte à la Parisienne* but soon changed the name to honor his then-employer, Tsar Alexander of Russia, who was living in the Elysée Palace at the time. Because of the tsar's presence, Russian dishes became very popular in Paris, and dinner service switched from "à la francaise" (lots of serving dishes placed all over the table) to "à la russe" (individual passed courses). Both the hot and the cold charlottes have the same shape. Carême's chilled, uncooked dessert, however, substitutes ladyfingers, which are sometimes soaked in liqueur or coffee, for the buttered toast; and the fruit purée is replaced with a Bavarian cream, mousse, flavored whipped cream, or a frozen bombe mixture. Sometimes additional ladyfingers or thin cake layers are intermixed with layers of the cold cream; or, for an even more elaborate presentation, several flavors of Bavarian cream are layered, resulting in multicolored stripes.

While the charlotte is a homey dish, the Charlotte Russe is fancier and lends itself to more ornate decoration—swirls of whipped cream, angelica cutouts, edible flowers, or chocolate shavings and drizzles. It is fun to let the decoration announce the filling: use fresh raspberries to decorate a raspberry Charlotte Russe, banana slices for a chocolate banana concoction, or candied lemon slices on a lemon dessert.

In New York starting in the mid-1800s, a simple version of the Charlotte Russe was made in individual portions and served at the local bakery or corner candy store. It was especially popular among urban Jews who called it "Charely Roose" or "Charlotte Roosh." A two-inch round of sponge cake was placed on cardboard and surrounded by a frilled cardboard holder about four inches high. Whipped cream filled the void and ended in a spiral topped with a maraschino cherry and sometimes chocolate sprinkles. As you ate the cream you pushed the dessert's cardboard base up from the bottom so you could get to every last bite of cake.

Serves 10 to 12

⅓ cup plus 2 tablespoons orange liqueur such as
  Grand Marnier, Cointreau, or Triple Sec
30 to 35 ladyfingers, about 4 inches long
  and 1 to 2 inches wide
2 large navel oranges
1 cup plus 1 tablespoon sugar
¼ teaspoon orange oil (optional)
1½ tablespoons (1½ packets) powdered gelatin
5 large eggs, separated, plus 2 yolks
  at room temperature
2 teaspoons cornstarch
1½ cups milk
Large pinch of salt
¼ teaspoon cream of tartar
½ cup very cold heavy cream

For the garnish (optional):
3 navel oranges, peeled and cut into supremes (orange
  segments cut between the membranes), mixed with 3
  tablespoons orange liqueur and sugar to taste
Whipped cream

1. Place a round of wax paper in the bottom of a
12-cup charlotte mold. In a shallow bowl, stir together ⅓
cup orange liqueur and ⅓ cup water. Quickly dip each
ladyfinger into the liqueur mixture and place on a wire
rack to drain.
2. Place a row of ladyfingers upright and fitted tightly
together, their curved sides against the sides of the mold.
Cut more ladyfingers to fit the bottom of the mold exactly
(and attractively). There should be ladyfingers left over
that you will use to cover the top once the mold has
been filled.
3. Finely zest 2 oranges and mix the zest with 1 cup
sugar and the orange oil, if using, and set aside.
4. Juice the zested oranges into a small bowl. Sprinkle
the gelatin over the juice. Set aside.
5. Using an electric mixer, beat the 7 egg yolks together
with the orange zest–sugar mixture until it is pale yellow
and forms a ribbon when dropped from the beaters,
about 5 minutes. Beat in the cornstarch.
6. In a medium-sized saucepan, bring the milk to a boil
and add it to the egg yolk mixture in a slow, steady
stream, continuing to beat.

7. Place the egg yolk mixture in the saucepan and cook
over medium heat, stirring constantly, until the mixture
thickens enough to coat the back of the spoon. Do not
boil the custard or the egg yolks will scramble. Remove
from the heat and immediately add the gelatin mixture,
stirring until the gelatin has completely dissolved.
8. Using an electric mixer fitted with the whisk attachment, beat the 5 reserved egg whites together with the
salt and cream of tartar until soft peaks form. Add the
remaining 1 tablespoon sugar and beat for another 30
seconds.
9. Fold the egg whites into the hot custard.
10. Place the bowl in an ice water bath to hasten the
cooling process. Stir occasionally until completely cooled.
11. When the custard is cool, whip the ½ cup cream
until soft peaks form.
12. When the custard is at room temperature and not
before, fold in the whipped cream and the remaining 2
tablespoons orange liqueur.
13. Pour into the lined mold and cover the top with the
remaining ladyfingers. Chill until set, at least 6 hours and
up to 2 days.
14. To unmold, run a sharp knife around the sides of the
mold. Invert onto a serving plate and remove the wax
paper. Refrigerate until ready to serve.
15. Cut into slices and serve with the orange segment
garnish and/or whipped cream, if desired.

Variation: I love this dessert's delicacy as is, but it is also
very good with the addition of candied orange peel,
which provides an extra hit of orange and the interest of
another (chewy) texture. Finely mince ½ cup candied
orange peel. Put one-third of the custard into the lined
mold, and sprinkle with half the minced candied peel.
Add another third of the custard, then sprinkle with the
rest of the minced peel. Add the last third of custard and
top with ladyfingers.

Note: This recipe uses raw egg whites. If you are concerned about bacteria, or if serving to the young, elderly,
or those with health issues, use pasteurized egg whites
or liquid egg whites as a substitute. Also, there's less risk
of bacteria with organic eggs.

Lemon Curd Mousse

IN ALMOND TUILE CUPS

Until it closed in the late 1990s, Arcadia, on Sixty-Second Street just east of Fifth Avenue, was my favorite New York City restaurant. It was co-owned by Anne Rosenzweig, who cooked, and Ken Aretsky (who had owned and run several other local restaurants). As Ruth Reichl said in a 1994 *New York Times* review of Arcadia, "When you walk out of the sunlight into this gracious flower-filled room, you leave the real world behind . . . the illusion of being outside of time and space is never shattered." Much of the atmosphere of sunny calm resulted from the charming, woodsy, Paul Davis mural that completely surrounded the dining room. In the introduction to her cookbook, Rosenzweig states that the food and the mural—and the restaurant itself—were inspired by the Hudson River Valley, "where the unspoiled hills, flowing streams, and rolling farmland look and smell and feel like Arcadia, the mythic Greek region of unfettered rustic simplicity and unblemished natural beauty." The mural stressed seasonality, as did the menu. The painting seamlessly segued from spring to summer, fall, winter, and back again to spring, all the while emanating a bucolic peacefulness that transported the viewer to an arcadian world, better and more expansive than the reality of the restaurant's narrow dining room. I loved Arcadia for its elegant simplicity combined with a certain coziness; but even more for the delicious American-classics-with-a-twist food. The savory dishes were top-notch; Rosenzweig later opened The Lobster Club, named after a savory—and much imitated—sandwich she became famous for inventing at Arcadia. But the highly satisfying, often very rich desserts represented Rosenzweig at her best.

The Lemon Curd Mousse is a whipped cream–lightened lemon curd served in delicate tuile cups, with colorful berries spilling out "as in a cornucopia." Deliciously creamy but still light (in taste if not in calories), this dessert is ethereal, a wonderful play of contrasts: the crisp, crunchy tuile a counterpoint to the soft, smooth mousse, its sweetness offset by the tang of lemon, and all finished with the pure, clean taste of fresh berries. The beautiful result is a festive, upbeat note on which to end a summer dinner. This recipe is adapted from Rosenzweig's lovely *Arcadia Seasonal Mural and Cookbook* (1986). I highly recommend both the book and the dessert. The book is small, having only one menu of recipes per season. The pages unfold, accordian-style, to reveal a running reproduction of the restaurant's spectacular wall mural of a lovely fantasy-driven Arcady.

Serves 6

2 large eggs, plus 2 large yolks
½ cup plus 1 tablespoon sugar
Pinch of salt
1 heaping tablespoon finely grated lemon zest
7 tablespoons fresh lemon juice
9 tablespoons unsalted butter, chilled and cut into
    little pieces
2 cups very cold heavy cream
6 Almond Tuile Cups (recipe follows)
2½ cups mixed fresh berries (raspberries, strawberries,
    blueberries, blackberries)

1. Whisk together the eggs, egg yolks, sugar, salt, lemon zest, and lemon juice in a medium-sized heavy-bottomed saucepan.

2. Cook over medium heat, stirring constantly while adding the butter pieces a few at a time.

3. Keep stirring until the mixture is very thick, but do not let it come to a simmer.

4. Remove from the heat and immediately pour into a ceramic or metal bowl. Place a piece of plastic wrap directly on the surface of the custard, poking a few holes in the plastic to release the steam. Let cool, then chill in the refrigerator until the lemon curd is very cold. The dessert can be made up to this point 5 days in advance if refrigerated; the lemon curd can be frozen for up to 3 months. If frozen, thaw before continuing.

5. Whip the cream until soft peaks form, then fold it into the lemon curd. Refrigerate the mousse (for up to 6 hours) if not eating immediately. When ready to serve, place the tuile cups on dessert plates and divide the mousse equally among them. Divide the berries evenly among the 6 portions, arranging them so they spill out, cornucopia-like.

ALMOND TUILE CUPS

Makes 8

2 tablespoons clarified butter
2 large eggs, at room temperature
6 tablespoons sugar
Pinch of salt
⅔ cup all-purpose flour
¾ cup sliced almonds

1. Preheat the oven to 375 degrees. Cover a large baking sheet with parchment paper and brush the paper liberally with some of the clarified butter, or even better, use a silicone baking sheet such as a Silpat and omit the butter.

2. Whisk the eggs in a bowl, then whisk in the sugar, salt, flour, and almonds in that order.

3. Using half the batter, make four 5-inch circles on the prepared baking sheet. Spread the batter very thinly (you may even have a few holes) so the tuiles will be delicate and crisp.

4. Bake for 10 to 15 minutes, until the tuiles are deep golden.

5. Using a metal spatula, remove the tuiles one by one and immediately (before they cool) shape them by fitting them into coffee cups. Let them cool.

6. Butter the parchment again, if using, and divide the rest of the batter to bake four more tuiles in the same manner.

Variation: This batter also makes delicious flat tuiles of any size. Once cooked, remove them immediately from the baking sheet and let them cool on a wire rack. Don't form them into cups.

Gooseberry Fool

The British have been making fruit fools since the 1500s. In Jane Grigson's classic, *Good Things* (1971), she writes that the word fool is taken from the French *fouler*, "to crush," and is not "a description of someone prepared to pay the [outrageous at the time] price of half a pint of cream." The earliest fools often contained eggs, other thickeners, spices, lemon peel, and wine, though with time it became apparent that these additions marred rather than enhanced the pure flavor of the fruit; soon fools came to mean nothing more than sweetened crushed or puréed fruit that was folded together with whipped cream just before serving.

The Gooseberry Fool was particularly popular during Queen Victoria's reign, and Grigson proclaims it to be as prototypically English as steak and kidney pie. Often the English steeped elderflowers with the gooseberries or added a few tablespoons of elderflower cordial. In the book *An Omelette and a Glass of Wine*, British food writer Elizabeth David writes, "I give precedence to those dishes made from green gooseberries because green gooseberry fool is—to me at any rate—the most delicious as well as the most characteristic of all these simple, almost childlike, English dishes." The gooseberry's elusive, somewhat haunting taste is unique, and its tartness is a nice foil to the rich cream.

I have adapted Grigson's recipe. She promotes using crushed, unsieved fruit to point up the texture of the gooseberries; but if smoother cream is preferred, push the purée through a sieve. Fools freeze well and make superb ice creams. If you plan to freeze the fool, definitely sieve the fruit or at least crush it well before incorporating the cream to avoid lumps of frozen fruit.

Strawberries (alone or combined with red currants), raspberries, peaches, plums, and nectarines all make delicious fools, as do cooked and puréed apples, pears, quinces, and stewed rhubarb. In the *The Accomplisht Cook* (1660), Robert May, who worked in the kitchens of a number of noble households, includes a recipe for a fool that he called "black tart stuff" made of prunes, raisins, and red wine or port.

Serves 6 to 8

1 pound fresh gooseberries, preferably young and green
    (see Note), topped and tailed
4 tablespoons (½ stick) unsalted butter
Pinch of salt
About ½ cup sugar, or more depending on the ripeness
    of the gooseberries
1½ cups very cold heavy cream, whipped to soft peaks
Additional fresh gooseberries or julienned organic rose
    petals for garnish (optional)

1. Put the gooseberries in a medium-sized saucepan with
the butter, salt, and ¼ cup of the sugar.
2. Cover and cook over very low heat until the gooseberries are just beginning to fall apart. Crush them with a
fork and add more sugar, if desired. (If they are green and
young, they will need extra sugar.)
3. Let cool completely, then fold the cooled gooseberries
into the whipped cream. Taste again and add sugar, if
desired. Refrigerate until ready to serve.
4. If possible, serve in glass or white ceramic bowls;
sprinkle the extra gooseberries or rose petals over the top,
if using.

Note: If gooseberries are unavailable, delicious fools can
be made with stewed and sweetened rhubarb; apple,
pear, or quince purée or a mixture; or with sweetened
uncooked raspberries, blackberries, peaches, plums, or
nectarines. Use equal parts purée or crushed fruit and
heavy cream (measured before whipping).

Marbled Rose and Raspberry Fool

This very beautiful and old-fashioned English dessert contains rose water, the most delicate of flavorings, which was popular in both Tudor and Stuart cookery. At the time, the consumption of the leaves, flowers, and hips of the rose plant was considered important for good health. Rose bushes were commonly grown in kitchen gardens alongside fruits, vegetables, and herbs.

A confetti of rose petals makes this pink-and-white marbled confection gorgeous and particularly festive. (Pink, red, white, or peach petals are lovely, and even better is a combination). If you can find them, *fraise de bois* also make an excellent garnish; you can even use them to replace the raspberries in the recipe itself. Or try regular strawberries, as all strawberries are delicious with roses. You can also decorate with lots of crushed meringue, in the style of the Fané on page 130.

In America's pre-Civil War South, fools were often served frozen. This one is excellent and dramatic frozen and unmolded onto a platter or large meringue, iced with a little sweetened whipped cream, and strewn with petals and raspberries.

Serves 8

2 pounds fresh or frozen raspberries
Pinch of salt
1¼ cups sugar, plus more for garnish (superfine
   is preferable)
2 cups very cold heavy cream
2 tablespoons rose water
½ cup julienned organic rose petals (optional) and/or
   ½ cup fresh raspberries rolled in sugar

1. Put half of the raspberries in a saucepan with the salt, ¾ cup of the sugar, and 2 tablespoons water.
2. Bring to a boil over medium heat. Lower the heat and simmer until the raspberries start to give off their juice, about 5 minutes. Push through a sieve, discarding the seeds, and let cool completely.
3. Whip the cream with the remaining ½ cup sugar until soft peaks form.
4. Mash the uncooked berries.
5. Fold the mashed uncooked berries and the rose water thoroughly into the whipped cream. Fold in the cooled cooked berries just enough to create a marbled effect. Refrigerate for at least 3 hours before serving; if possible, serve from a glass bowl and into glass cups or dessert bowls. Decorate with the julienned rose petals and/or the berries rolled in sugar.

Variation: To serve frozen, freeze in a metal bowl or charlotte mold and then dip in a larger bowl of very hot water for 15 seconds or so and unmold. If the fool does not unmold easily, dip in the hot water for a few seconds more and unmold onto a serving plate or onto a meringue base (see page 130). Let the unmolded frozen fool soften for at least fifteen minutes at room temperature. Garnish with more whipped cream and sprinkle with rose petals and sugared berries and, if you'd like, serve this frozen version with Raspberry Sauce (page 190) to which 1 or 2 tablespoons of rose water has been added.

Salammbos

A noteworthy dessert, the Salammbo (described next page) is the most lost of a number of traditional and now uncommon choux paste confections.

LA RELIGIEUSE (THE NUN). When Marie Leszczynski, daughter of Poland's King Stanislas (an amateur baker himself and, according to George Lang, inventor of the *baba au rhum*), arrived in Paris in 1725 to marry Louis XV, she brought along her father's pastry chef, Monsieur Stohrer. Five years later he opened a tiny pastry shop on the rue Montorgueil near Les Halles. It remains there to this day, the oldest and possibly most charming pâtisserie in *le tout Paris*. Among other claims to fame, Stohrer created the original *la religieuse*. Choux paste was made into éclairs—filled with chocolate or coffee pastry cream—which were then stacked on top of one another or arranged in a pyramid on a base of sweet pastry. In a later version, a large choux pastry was similarly filled with coffee or chocolate pastry cream and surmounted by smaller cream puffs; the whole was iced with fondant, the same flavor as the filling and decorated with piped buttercream. The dessert is thought to have been named "la religieuse" because it is the color of homespun robes worn by nuns.

PARIS-BREST. The person who invented the Paris-Brest remains unknown, but we do know that the dessert was created in 1891 by a pastry chef whose shop in the Paris suburbs was on the route of the bicycle race between Paris and Brest. The dessert is a large choux paste cake shaped like a bicycle wheel, filled with praline-flavored pastry cream and sprinkled with slivered almonds. There is a lesser-known version called Paris-Nice that is filled with Saint-Honoré cream and has no nuts.

GÂTEAU SAINT-HONORÉ. Named after the patron saint of bakers and pastry chefs, this dessert shares its name with the Parisian street on which its creator, the patissière Chiboust, had his shop. First made in 1846, the cake consists of a round puff pastry crust on top of which is arranged a bordering circle of choux paste, garnished with little caramel-glazed choux paste balls. The inside of the circle is filled with Chiboust cream (also known as Saint-Honoré cream, it is vanilla pastry cream lightened while still warm with stiffly beaten egg whites) or chantilly (whipped cream). Gâteau Saint-Honoré is still frequently seen in Parisian patisseries, but the use of Chiboust's cream is essentially lost. The dessert these days is usually made with a regular, heavier pastry cream.

The original Salammbo was an elegant affair, a large oval cream puff, the filling perfumed with Grand Marnier and the top a beautiful translucent, amber-like hard caramel sprinkled with chopped pistachio nuts. In the one Salammbo recipe I could find, the famous French pasty chef Gaston Lenôtre substituted rum for the Grand Marnier and eliminated the pistachios. A very pedestrian version of this dessert, nicknamed *les grenouilles* (frogs) by French schoolchildren, and commonly found in modern-day pâtisseries, is covered with bright green icing and chocolate sprinkles and filled with heavy, Kirsch-flavored cream. Luckily, neither Lenôtre's recipe nor the classic one is anything like the garish "frogs."

Salammbos were invented in 1890 and named for Ernest Reyer's hit opera *Salammbô*. First produced that same year, it was based on his friend Gustave Flaubert's colorful 1862 piece of historical fiction, which took place in Carthage between the two Punic Wars. The opera features the princess-turned-pagan-priestess Salammbô. The sets were sumptuous and the plot turgid. (A memorable incident—in the novel, at least, and quite risqué for the time—is Salammbô's erotic encounter with a python.)

Makes 24 cream puffs

For the choux paste:
¼ cup (½ stick) unsalted butter, cut into 4 pieces
¼ teaspoon salt
1 teaspoon granulated sugar
½ cup all-purpose flour
2 large eggs, at room temperature, plus an additional egg
    if necessary
⅛ teaspoon orange extract
Confectioners' sugar, for dusting

For the pastry cream:
2 cups milk
½ vanilla bean, split and scraped
Large pinch of salt
6 large egg yolks
⅔ cup sugar
¼ cup cornstarch or all-purpose flour
2 to 3 tablespoons unsalted butter (optional)
2 tablespoons dark rum or Grand Marnier, or more to taste

For the caramel:
1 cup sugar
½ teaspoon fresh lemon juice
½ cup finely chopped toasted pistachios (optional)

To make the choux paste:
1. Put the butter, salt, granulated sugar, and 1 cup water in a 2-quart saucepan.
2. Bring to a rolling boil over medium heat. When the butter is completely melted, remove the pan from the heat and add the flour all at once. With a large wooden spoon, quickly stir in the flour; the mixture will be the consistency of mashed potatoes.
3. Return the pan to medium heat. Mix the paste vigorously for 1 to 2 minutes, until it becomes a smooth, doughy mass that no longer sticks to the pan or spoon and moves all together with the spoon when stirred. Remove from the heat.
4. Transfer the dough to the bowl of an electric mixer fitted with the paddle attachment. Make an indentation in the center of the dough before it begins to cool. Break an egg into the indentation and turn on the mixer. After the first few strokes, the paste will separate into moist, doughy strands. Continue to beat vigorously until the dough comes together again and forms a solid mass. Make another indentation in the dough and add the second egg. Beat as before. (You can use a wooden spoon and do this by hand but it is hard going.)

5. After the second egg has been incorporated, the dough should be smooth and shiny and should fall lazily back into the bowl off the lifted spoon. If the paste is too firm and resistant, break another egg into a dish, stir it lightly with a fork, then beat one quarter to half of it into the paste to give it the proper consistency.

6. Beat in the orange extract.

7. Preheat the oven to 450 degrees. Butter and flour two large baking sheets or line them with parchment paper.

8. Use soup spoons to make mounds of dough about 1 inch wide, 2 inches long, ¾ inch high and spaced about 1½ inches apart. Don't fuss too much. It is fine if they are a bit irregular. The dough is sticky, and this process is facilitated by lightly buttering the spoons before starting and then dipping them in flour before forming each puff. If you are handy with a pastry bag, by all means use it. You will get more uniform pastries. Dust the mounds with confectioners' sugar so their shapes will be more even after baking.

9. Bake for 5 minutes, then lower the oven temperature to 425 degrees and bake for an additional 10 minutes. Lower the heat to 400 degrees and bake until done, 5 to 10 minutes more. The puffs should be golden brown, free of external moisture, and not doughy inside. Cut one in half horizontally to check; if it is not ready, pierce one side of each puff with a sharp knife and cook for a few minutes longer. Turn off the oven and leave the puffs inside for 10 minutes. Remove from the oven and let cool completely on a wire rack. Cut another puff in half to test. The puffs should be light and airy. If the sample puff is still heavy and doughy when you cut it in half, cut the rest of the puffs in half, remove the extra dough from the insides with your fingers, and place the puffs, cut side up, on a baking sheet in a 250-degree oven to dry them out before cooling on a wire rack. The baked puffs, wrapped airtight, will keep for 1 week in the refrigerator or at least 2 months in the freezer.

To make the pastry cream:

1. Place the milk, vanilla bean and its seeds, and salt in a small saucepan. Bring almost to a boil, then remove from the heat and cover.

2. Using an electric mixer fitted with the whisk attachment, beat the egg yolks together with the sugar on medium speed until the mixture lightens and forms a ribbon when dropped from the beaters, about 5 minutes using an electric mixer. Gently stir in the cornstarch or flour.

3. Reheat the milk if it has cooled, and pass it through a sieve. While whisking, gradually add the hot milk to the egg and sugar mixture. Pour the mixture back into the saucepan and bring to a boil, stirring constantly with a wire whisk to prevent burning. Boil for 1 minute, continuing to whisk.

4. Pour into a bowl and dot the surface with butter or cover with plastic wrap or foil directly touching the surface to keep a skin from forming.

5. When almost cool, stir in the rum. Let cool completely, then refrigerate if not using immediately.

To make the caramel and to glaze the puffs:

1. When the puffs are completely cooled, butter two baking sheets.

2. Heat the sugar, the lemon juice, and 6 tablespoons water in a small skillet (the low sides make dipping easier than using a saucepan). Stir until the sugar dissolves, then boil until the caramel is a very dark honey color; a candy thermometer should read 375 degrees. Remove from the heat.

3. Quickly, before the caramel cools, dip the top of each puff in the caramel and place it, caramel side down, on the buttered baking sheet. If the caramel cooks and hardens in the pan before you have finished, re-melt it gently over a low heat. If there is extra caramel, dip the puffs a second time to get a really thick hard caramel layer on top. The thick caramel is beautiful and looks like amber. (If you want to use the pistachios, while the cramel topping on the puffs is still warm and sticky, dip the ends of each puff in the chopped pistachios, pat if necessary to encourage adherence, then place the puff, caramel and pistachio side down, on the baking sheet to cool.) Once cool, the cream puffs are ready to fill.

To fill the puffs:

1. Preferably no more than 1 hour before serving, cut the cream puffs in half horizontally with a sharp knife and remove any doughy bits with your fingers if you haven't done so already. Put a large spoonful of pastry cream on the lower half, then replace the carameled top. (Or use a pastry bag fitted with a ⅛-inch tip. Poke a hole in the bottom of each puff with a small knife, insert the pastry tip, and fill with the pastry cream.)

Notes: This recipe makes 24 3-by-4-inch cream puffs.

The baked uncaramelized puffs will keep 1 week in the refrigerator and at least 2 months in the freezer.

Sauternes Bavarian Cream

A Bavarian is a cold, traditionally unmolded cream, often flavored with fruit purée or nuts and sometimes with liqueur. It is distinguished from other mousse-type desserts by the addition of gelatin and is composed of two parts: the first, whipped cream and beaten egg whites, is folded into the second, a gelatin-stiffened egg custard. The result is a stable and unmoldable dessert that is also light and airy. Though classically made in large tube molds with fancy shapes, a more delicate version uses less gelatin and is not unmolded. Made in one large portion or individual ones, this version is customarily served from crystal or glass bowls, or from silver timbales, often garnished with piped whipped cream, chocolate shavings, candied or edible fresh flowers, or glacéed fruits.

The dessert was developed in the late seventeenth or early eighteenth century by French chefs working in Bavaria for the Wittelsbach princes; they learned how to make or created Bavarian cream there and brought it back to France. Antonin Carême gives dozens of recipes for what he called "fromages bavarois." Especially noteworthy is one flavored with green walnuts that he created in 1817 for the prince regent at his splendid Orientalist, John Nash–renovated Brighton Pavilion.

The Bavarian, with rare exception, has been out of favor for a long time. As far back as 1934, when giving a recipe for it in *Ma Cuisine*, Auguste Escoffier said, "This sweet is seldom used today as it has been replaced by creams and mousses. . . ." The following is adapted from that Escoffier recipe. Use Sauternes, Muscat, Beaumes-de-Venise, or any other rich, sweet dessert wine. The Bavarian is sensational when accompanied by a glass of the same wine used to make it, and served with a fruit sauce, a coulis, a combination of fresh fruit, or caramelized fruit such as peaches or nectarines. Also amusing is to decorate it with thin slices of fresh or candied fruit as Eric and I did for this photograph. The decoration will adhere better if the Bavarian is first iced with a thin layer of whipped cream.

Serves 8 to 10

1½ cups plus 2 tablespoons whole milk
½ vanilla bean, split and scraped
1 scant cup sugar
Large pinch of salt
8 large egg yolks
4 teaspoons (1⅓ packets) powdered gelatin, dissolved in
    2 tablespoons water
¾ cup Sauternes, Vin Santo, Muscat, or other sweet
    dessert wine
2½ cups very cold heavy cream, whipped

1. Grease an 8- to 10-cup mold or 8 to 10 individual
1-cup molds with a tasteless vegetable oil such as
canola.
2. Put the milk and the vanilla bean with its seeds in a
medium-sized saucepan. Bring to a boil, turn off the heat,
cover, and set aside to steep.
3. Using an electric mixer, beat the sugar, salt, and egg
yolks together until very light and creamy, about 5
minutes, scraping the bowl occasionally with a rubber
spatula.
4. Return the milk to a simmer. Off the heat, stir in the
dissolved gelatin and slowly add the liquid back to the
egg yolk mixture, beating constantly.
5. Put the mixture back in the saucepan and cook over
low heat, stirring, until the mixture is thick enough to
coat the back of a spoon; do not boil.
6. Pour the mixture through a sieve into a bowl, stir, and let
cool. When cool, stir in the dessert wine. When the mixture
begins to set up, stir again. Then fold in the whipped
cream and pour into the prepared mold(s). Refrigerate
until set, at least 4 hours.
7. When ready to serve, dab the top of the Bavarian(s)
dry with a paper towel, and turn out onto a serving dish
or individual plates. If you have trouble unmolding, dip
the mold(s) in hot water for 15 seconds and try again;
repeat if necessary.

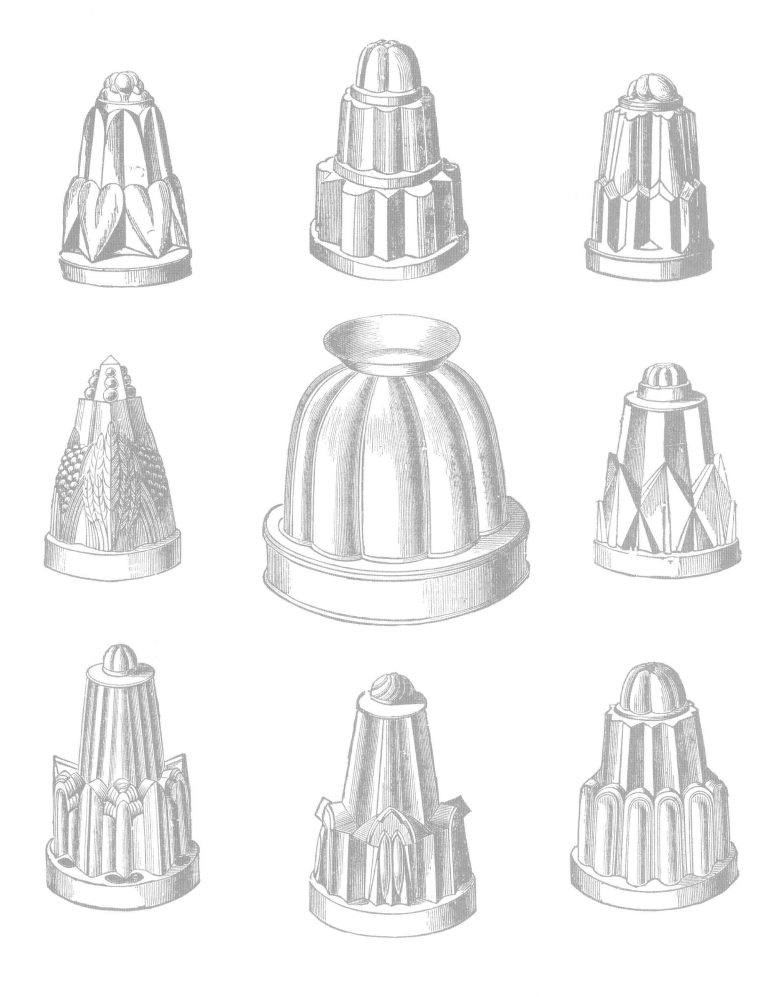

PUDDINGS
and JELLIES

Caramelized Rice Pudding with Ginger

Queen of Puddings

Lady Agnes Jekyll's Old-Fashioned Orange Jelly

Sticky Toffee Pudding

Gingerbread and Pear Upside-down Pudding

Villa Bellosguardo's Chocolate Pudding

Red Wine Jelly

Arcadia's Chocolate Bread Pudding
with Brandy Custard Sauce

Caramelized Rice Pudding

WITH GINGER

Rice pudding is quintessential comfort food in many parts of the world. Although the East Asians have eaten it in many forms for thousands of years, our Western variety originated in Persia and migrated to the Iberian Peninsula sometime during the Moorish occupation. There it morphed into *arroz con miel* but did not really gain permanent popularity until the Middle Ages. By the nineteenth century, rice pudding was common fare throughout much of Europe. In Eliza Acton's *Modern Cookery for Private Families* (1855), which preeminent British food writer Elizabeth David called "the greatest cookery book in our language," Acton gives us no less than seven versions; Fannie Farmer includes four; and in *Ma Cuisine*, Auguste Escoffier includes three. More recently, in *Classic Home Desserts*, Richard Sax gives us nine.

Most rice desserts from years past are now rarely prepared. Two of the most elaborate and well-known ones, *riz à l'impératrice* and *riz à la Condé*, were created by Antonin Carême in the early 1800s. The former was invented to honor Empress Josephine, the latter the Prince de Condé. Both are rich and heavy with candied and fresh fruit, custard, and liquor.

Another, lesser known, is *tête de negre*, an eccentric rice dessert most likely lost because of its politically incorrect name; however, this chocolate blackamoor head is impressive and worth making. If you want to give it a try, make the basic rice pudding as in the following recipe but omit the fresh and candied gingers, and double the vanilla extract. Do not caramelize the mold. Instead, once the pudding has chilled and been unmolded, make a chocolate glaze by melting six ounces of semisweet chocolate with eight tablespoons of butter and one tablespoon of water. Completely cover the cold unmolded pudding with the hot chocolate sauce, which will harden as it cools. Chill again. To serve, whip two cups of heavy cream and pile on top like a turban.

The following traditional French rice pudding is made in a caramel-lined mold and then inverted in the manner of *crème renversée au caramel*. The dish combines the nurture of comfort food with the elegance of an unmolded dessert, beautiful and glistening. The addition of ginger is mine, but if you prefer, omit it and use the more traditional raisins, lemon zest, vanilla, and cinnamon instead. Though less unusual, it is equally satisfying.

Serves 8

1⅓ cups sugar
3½ cups whole milk
2 cups heavy cream
¼ scant teaspoon salt
1 (2-inch) cinnamon stick
Finely grated zest of 1 large lemon
2 inches fresh ginger, peeled and cut into 4 (½-inch)
    rounds
¾ cup long-grain white rice, rinsed in cold water
3 large eggs, separated, at room temperature
2 teaspoons vanilla extract
⅓ cup finely diced crystallized ginger, sugar rinsed off,
    drained and dried

1. In a 12-cup ovenproof saucepan over medium heat, cook 1 cup of the sugar with ½ cup water, stirring until the sugar dissolves. Cook the syrup undisturbed, until the caramel is a very deep honey color (about 375 degrees). Remove the pan from the heat. Let cool for one minute, until the syrup thickens enough to coat the sides of the pan. Tilt the pan so that the bottom and sides are covered in caramel (alternately line a 12-cup metal or ceramic casserole or bundt pan by immediately pouring in the hot caramel and tilting the pan to coat). Set the caramelized pan or mold aside until needed.
2. Preheat the oven to 350 degrees.
3. Place the milk, ½ cup of the cream, the salt, the remaining ⅓ cup sugar, cinnamon stick, lemon zest, and fresh ginger in a medium-sized saucepan. Bring the mixture to a boil, turn down the heat, and simmer for 2 minutes.
4. Add the rice and simmer, stirring frequently, until quite soft, about 20 minutes.
5. Remove from the heat and let cool to lukewarm. Remove the ginger rounds and the cinnamon stick.

6. Beat the egg yolks together with the vanilla and add to the cooled rice mixture.
7. Stir in the candied ginger.
8. Using an electic mixer fitted with the whisk attachment, beat the egg whites until soft peaks form. Stir one quarter of the egg whites into the rice mixture, then fold in the rest.
9. Spoon the rice mixture into the caramelized mold and bake in a bain marie (a larger pan with hot water that comes halfway up the sides of the mold) in the middle of the oven until set, about 1 to 1½ hours.
10. Remove from the oven and let cool for 2 hours, then invert the pudding onto a serving plate, tapping the mold and the plate together sharply against the counter. If the pudding sticks a bit when unmolding, use a spatula to remove the stuck parts and place them on the pudding. To hide the imperfections, you can whip the remaining 1½ cups cream and dollop it on top of the pudding before serving.
11. Serve with unsweetened whipped cream or a pitcher of heavy cream.

Variations: Instead of caramelizing the mold, create a beautiful clear and crackly caramel coating. To do this, butter the mold very heavily instead of caramelizing it. After the pudding is unmolded and cool, make a syrup using 2 cups sugar and 1 cup water, as in step 1. When you have a nice dark caramel, immediately but slowly pour it carefully and evenly over the pudding. Serve within a couple of hours after the caramel has cooled; otherwise the caramel may soften, which is fine but you will lose the fabulous crackle. Another variation is to omit the fresh and the candied ginger. If you double the amounts of cinnamon and lemon zest, and add a generous grating of nutmeg, you will have a delicious, more traditionally flavored rice pudding.

Queen of Puddings

The royal reference here is to Queen Victoria—and the dessert is also known as the queen's pudding. Though created in the Buckingham Palace kitchens during Victoria's reign, the pudding was based on much earlier recipes; it combined a seventeenth-century nursery food—milk pudding thickened with bread crumbs and eggs (sometimes baked in a puff pastry case)—with non-nursery antecedents such as tipsy pudding, trifle pudding, and the very rich cabinet pudding. The first two contained spirits and the last incorporated chopped candied fruits, sponge cake, and ratafia biscuits (cookies containing ratafia essence, a flavoring made from bitter almonds or the kernels inside peach pits).

Queen of Puddings became popular in America's antebellum South and was included in *Mrs. Hill's New Cook Book* (1867) written "by Mrs. A. P. Hill, widow of Hon. Edward Y. Hill, of Georgia." She dedicated the book to "young and inexperienced Southern housekeepers," women who were raised before the Civil War and had never needed to set foot in a kitchen. Versions of this pudding appeared all through the post–Civil War South with patriotic names such as "Dixie," "Jeff Davis," and "Secession."

This dessert is a favorite of my British friends Tessa Traeger and Patrick Kinmouth. For years Tessa was food photographer for British *Vogue* and first discovered the dessert while working with the magazine's Arabella Boxer on an English food cookbook. Appropriately, I tasted Queen of Puddings for the first time while staying with Tessa and Patrick at Cory, their spectacular medieval manor house in Devon. I was in good company. Apparently, Charles II had also stayed at Cory on his way back to London to be "Restored." It is perfectly plausible that while there, he too sampled a version of this splendid custard, bread, jam, and meringue creation.

Serves 6

For the pudding:
8 ounces slightly stale white bread, cut into ½-inch cubes
½ cup sugar
4 cups whole milk
Pinch of salt
6 tablespoons unsalted butter
Finely grated zest of 2 lemons
8 large eggs, separated (reserve 4 whites at room
     temperature for the meringue)
¼ cup strawberry, raspberry, or apricot jam

For the meringue:
4 large egg whites (reserved from the pudding)
½ teaspoon fresh lemon juice
½ teaspoon vanilla extract
1 cup plus 1 teaspoon sugar

To make the pudding:
1. Butter a 9- or 10-inch square baking dish, or an oval gratin dish 9 to 10 inches long, and sprinkle the bread cubes evenly over the bottom.
2. Put the sugar, milk, salt, butter, and lemon zest in a medium saucepan and bring to a boil. Turn off the heat, cover, and let steep for 30 minutes.
3. Beat the 8 egg yolks and stir them into the lukewarm milk mixture.
4. Pass the liquid through a sieve over the bread and push the cubes down with a large spoon to be sure they are all submerged. Let the bread soak up the liquid for at least 20 minutes or up to 2 hours.
5. Preheat the oven to 350 degrees.
6. Put the baking dish in a bain marie (a larger pan with hot water that comes halfway up the sides of the baking dish) and bake until lightly set, about 25 minutes. Remove from the oven but leave the oven on.
7. Warm the jam in a small saucepan and spread it over the baked custard. Set aside.

To make the meringue:
1. Using an electric mixer fitted with the whisk attachment, beat the 4 egg whites until foamy. Beat in the lemon juice and vanilla and slowly increase the speed. When the egg whites form very soft peaks, very gradually add 1 cup of the sugar and beat at high speed until the meringue forms glossy, stiff peaks.
2. Dollop the meringue over the jam making sure all of the jam is covered. Sprinkle with the remaining 1 teaspoon sugar. Bake at 350 degrees until the meringue peaks are lightly browned, about 20 minutes.
3. Serve warm with heavy cream or Jam Sauce (see recipe below), or serve cold with fresh berries.

JAM SAUCE

Makes approximately 1 cup

1 cup apricot, strawberry, or raspberry jam
1 tablespoon sugar
Small pinch of salt
Fresh lemon juice to taste (about 1 teaspoon)
2 tablespoons brandy, Kirsch, or rum

1. Put the jam, sugar, salt, and ½ cup cold water in a small saucepan. Bring to a boil, then lower the heat and simmer for 5 minutes, stirring constantly.
2. Pour the sauce through a sieve placed over a bowl and use a large spoon to push it through.
3. Stir in the lemon juice and brandy and set aside until ready to use or cover and refrigerate indefinitely.
4. Bring to room temperature before using. If necessary, thin with more lemon juice or brandy.

Old-Fashioned Orange Jelly

In the 1700s, delicious wine and fruit jellies, often served with whipped cream, replaced the bright blue, orange, green, and red gelatin concoctions of the previous century. This Orange Jelly, adapted from Lady Agnes Jekyll's *Kitchen Essays* (1922), is typical. Lady Jekyll was the sister-in-law of the famous garden designer Gertrude Jekyll, whose biographer wrote that if Gertrude "was an artist-gardener, then Agnes was an artist-housekeeper." The book comprises Lady Jekyll's collected pieces for the *London Times* with names like "For Men Only," "For the Punctual and Unpunctual," and "Meatless Meals"; many of her ideas were far ahead of their time. In the chapter "A Supper after the Play," Jekyll writes, "For sweets, nothing is nicer than this specially good Orange Jelly. Not that stiffly moulded, colourless, and acid variety so usually and deservedly rejected, but soft and shapeless, of the colour of a blood orange, and really tasting of the fruit served in a shallow glass dish and accompanied by another dish containing a fresh Compote of Oranges made in the approved way, the fruit uncooked, all pit and pith removed, and a hot syrup of sugar and juice poured over the orange segments and allowed to cool."

This delicate Orange Jelly is an adaptation of Lady Jekyll's, and there is no resemblance to the hated mini-marshmallow-embellished overly dense and artifically flavored instant Jell-O of 1950s America. You can suspend thin lemon or orange slices, berries, currants, or other small pieces of fruit in this jelly—just slip them in when it is thickened but not completely set. I like to serve a bowl of whipped cream on the side, along with Lady Jekyll's crispy caramel biscuits (recipe follows).

Serves 4 to 6

5 large oranges (blood oranges, if you can find them)
1 lemon
$\frac{1}{2}$ cup sugar
2 tablespoons (2 packets) powdered gelatin dissolved in
$\quad$ $\frac{1}{2}$ cup water (see Notes)

1. Finely grate the zest of 1 of the oranges and the lemon into a bowl.
2. Squeeze the juice of all the oranges and the lemon and pour into the bowl with the zests.
3. Place the sugar and $1\frac{1}{4}$ cups water in a medium-sized saucepan and bring to a boil, stirring. Once the sugar has dissolved, boil until reduced by half.
4. Add the juices and zests and bring to a boil again. Skim well and add $1\frac{1}{4}$ cups more water. Bring to a boil again. Skim. Boil for 1 minute. The liquid should measure exactly $2\frac{1}{2}$ cups. Add water or boil to reduce to the correct amount.
5. Add the gelatin and stir until dissolved.
6. Pass the jelly through a sieve into a 3- or 4-cup mold or bowl (a heatproof glass bowl is beautiful if the jelly is to be served at the table). Let cool, then cover and refrigerate.

Notes: If you want to unmold the jelly, use 3 tablespoons (3 packets) gelatin. It will still be delicious, but its delicacy will be slightly compromised.

Lady Jekyll made her caramel biscuits by rolling puff pastry (using a good frozen brand is fine) to a $\frac{3}{16}$-inch thickness. Roll in abundant granulated sugar (vanilla sugar is even better, see page 191) instead of flour. Cut the pastry in 8-by-3-inch strips and place on a parchment-lined cookie sheet. Sprinkle generously with more sugar and bake in a preheated 350-degree oven until the cookies are dark golden and blistered, about 15 minutes. Cool on a rack. Store in an airtight container for up to 1 week.

Sticky Toffee Pudding

During a chilly August a number of years ago I traversed Scotland by train. Ogling the country-side through the window, playing cards, and eating were major pastimes. The food on the *Royal Scotsman* was superb—better than at most of the best restaurants in London let alone Edinburgh. The dishes were not particularly complicated, but the ingredients were fresh and of the highest quality, and whoever was cooking in the galley was amazing. One meal was better than the next. Even the components of afternoon tea—the scones, the clotted cream, the lemon and mixed berry tartlets, the Scottish shortbread—were some of the best I had ever eaten.

But my most vivid food memory from the trip was having Sticky Toffee Pudding for the first time. I had never seen it on a menu in the United States. The combination of gooey, chewy, slightly burnt caramel sauce over moist, puddingy cake (or cakey pudding), flavored with a mysterious mélange of coffee, vanilla, and chopped dates (the parts being unrecognizable in the whole), jolted me out of the lovely hypnotic stupor of train travel.

This is a traditional British dessert of the sort one rarely finds nowadays. British food writer Arabella Boxer calls it "the best of all the hot, rich English puddings, perfect for a weekend lunch party on a winter day." It is also good in the late fall and after dinner. It is not for hot summer—or even spring, for that matter—when a fruit tart, a refreshing ice cream or sorbet, or a fresh berry compote would be more welcome. Save it for cashmere-scarf, earmuff, and fire-in-the-fireplace weather.

The day I arrived back in New York from Scotland, I rushed out to purchase a number of cookbooks containing recipes for the dessert. By the next evening I had tried several. The one I give here (with a few changes) came from *Delia Smith's Christmas*.

Serves 8

For the pudding:
2 cups chopped, pitted dates
¾ cup boiling water
1 teaspoon vanilla extract
2 teaspoons instant espresso powder, such as Medaglia D'Oro

¾ teaspoon baking soda
6 tablespoons unsalted butter, at room temperature
½ cup plus 3 tablespoons sugar
2 large eggs, at room temperature
1¼ cups all-purpose flour
1¼ teaspoons baking powder
¼ teaspoon salt

For the sauce:
1 cup minus 2 tablespoons dark brown sugar
2 tablespoons unsalted butter
Small pinch of salt
6 tablespoons heavy cream
¼ cup chopped, toasted walnuts or almonds
Vanilla ice cream or very cold heavy cream

To make the puddings:
1. Place the dates in a bowl and pour the boiling water over them. Stir in the vanilla, instant espresso powder, and baking soda; set aside.
2. Preheat the oven to 350 degrees and lightly butter eight 6-ounce ramekins.
3. Using an electric mixer, cream the butter and sugar well. Add the eggs, one at a time. Continue beating until light and fluffy, about 5 minutes, scraping down the sides of the bowl frequently with a rubber spatula.
4. Sift the flour together with the baking powder and salt and partially fold into the egg mixture. Add the date mixture and fold gently until completely combined. The batter will be very wet.
5. Divide the batter equally among the prepared ramekins. Place the ramekins on a baking sheet and bake

in the middle of the oven for 20 minutes.
6. Let cool for 5 minutes. Run a small knife around each pudding to loosen, then invert each one into a shallow baking dish or onto a baking sheet. *Note:* The cooled puddings can be refrigerated well-wrapped for 3 days and frozen for three months. If frozen, thaw before using.

To make the sauce:
1. Place the brown sugar, butter, salt, and cream in a medium-sized saucepan. Bring to a simmer over medium heat, while stirring constantly. Simmer for 2 minutes until the sugar is dissolved, then set aside. Sauce can be refrigerated for up to 2 months. Reheat to use.

To serve:
1. Preheat the broiler to high and pour ⅔ of the sauce evenly over the puddings. Pour the rest of the sauce into a small pitcher. Broil the puddings about 5 inches from the heat until the tops are brown and crunchy and the sauce bubbling hot. Watch carefully: do not let them burn. Transfer the puddings to individual serving plates. Spoon any extra sauce left on the baking sheet over the puddings and sprinkle the nuts on top. Serve with the reserved sauce and the vanilla ice cream or heavy cream.

Gingerbread and Pear Upside-down Pudding

Once the weather turns cold, this combination of moist gingerbread and autumn fruit is the perfect dessert—the ideal finale for a tailgate picnic, a kitchen supper, or an informal dinner with friends. It is quite beautiful in a homey sort of way, the cooked pears shining like large medieval cabochon jewels set into the siena brown cake. Served warm with heavy cream, custard sauce, or vanilla ice cream on the side, this Victorian "pudding" is archetypal comfort food.

Gingerbread arrived in Europe during the Middle Ages. Crusaders returned from the Middle East laden with exotic spices, sugars, almonds, and citrus fruits. Catholic monks began making gingerbread for saints' days and festivals, and it was soon associated with Christmas. The expensive ingredients and high cost of running the ovens initally made it a treat only for the wealthy. Gradually, the exotic ingredients became less so, their prices dropped, and various forms of gingerbread became popular throughout Europe: Germans made a honeyed version called *lebkuchen*; Italians made hard, nut-filled *panforte*; and Burgundians made yeast-risen *pain d'epices*.

Nowhere was gingerbread as popular as in Colonial America. In her 1796 cookbook, *American Cookery*, Amelia Simmons included five different kinds. It was omnipresent in Britain also; in 1845 Eliza Acton gave six different recipes for this beloved dessert in her *Modern Cooking for Private Families*.

Serves 6 to 8

½ cup (1 stick) unsalted butter
¾ cup firmly packed brown sugar
Salt
3 firm, ripe pears
½ cup molasses
¼ cup golden syrup, such as Lyle's
1½ cups all-purpose flour
½ teaspoon instant espresso powder, such as
    Medaglia D'Oro
Large pinch of ground cloves
2 teaspoons ground cinnamon
1 tablespoon ground ginger
¼ teaspoon freshly grated nutmeg
⅔ cup whole milk
1¼ teaspoons baking soda
2 large eggs, at room temperature
Whipped cream or vanilla ice cream

1. Preheat the oven to 350 degrees. Butter the sides and bottom of an 8-inch round cake pan. Line the bottom with parchment paper and butter the paper.
2. Melt ¼ cup (half) of the butter in a small saucepan. Add ½ cup of the brown sugar and a pinch of salt, and cook over low heat, stirring, until the sugar is dissolved.
3. Pour the mixture into the prepared pan. Spread evenly.

4. Peel, halve vertically, and core the pears. Arrange the pear halves in a circle in the pan, cut side down, with their stem ends facing the center of the pan.
5. Put the remaining ¼ cup butter, the remaining ¼ cup brown sugar, the molasses, and golden syrup in a medium-sized saucepan and melt over medium-low heat.
6. Sift the flour, ¼ teaspoon salt, espresso powder, and spices together into a mixing bowl.
7. Heat the milk to lukewarm in a medium saucepan. Dissolve the baking soda in the warm milk.
8. Beat the eggs and add them to the milk mixture. Whisk in the molasses mixture.
9. Whisk the liquids into the flour mixture. Combine well, but do not overmix. Pour over the pears in the pan.
10. Bake in the center of the oven until well risen and a cake tester inserted into the center comes out clean, about 1 hour and 20 minutes. Let cool for 10 minutes, then invert onto a cake plate. Serve warm, with whipped cream or vanilla ice cream.

Notes: The cake can be made earlier in the day or up to 24 hours in advance, then reheated for 10 minutes in a 300-degree oven before turning out onto a serving plate.

If you really love ginger, fold one-third cup of finely minced candied ginger into the batter before putting it in the pan to bake.

Chocolate Pudding

Villa Bellosguardo is a magical hotel on a hill overlooking Florence. Its frequently published, picture-perfect garden is even more magical. There are flowers galore—lilacs, hydrangeas, camellias, and roses of all kinds. In summer, peach, apricot, and plum trees are laden with fruit. An immaculate kitchen garden boasts of every heirloom and modern herb imaginable. The grounds contain what must be one of the first "infinity" pools: an ornate affair, probably from the 1930s, partly shaded by old cypresses, and set in a green velvet lawn running straight off the edge of a steep cliff. While swimming, one has an unobstructed view of the Duomo and of the ancient corals, reds, and ochres of *tutto Firenze* spread out below.

I spent a college summer at the villa long before it became a hotel. I was disappointed during a recent visit to find there was nothing to eat except breakfast and a few simple snacks by the pool. This was not necessarily a hardship as there were plenty of tempting restaurants in Florence, an easy fifteen-minute walk down the hill. The problem was that I remembered elaborate dinners served every night in the villa's sixteenth-century dining room—endless courses passed on silver trays by processions of white-gloved waiters. I was especially eager to retaste Bellosguardo's fabulous Chocolate Pudding, unusually rich and silky and refreshingly not too sweet. Unmolded onto a shining platter in the kitchen, the dessert arrived at table elegant, old-fashioned, and with almost as much piped whipped cream on top—the sweetened cream being particularly good with the almost bitter taste of the chocolate—as there was pudding underneath.

I came home determined to re-create this dessert. It is great comfort food for the child in all of us. Ideally, it's for fall and winter; make it then, and you will feel nurtured and loved (even if only by yourself).

Serves 6 to 8

7 tablespoons unsalted butter
1 cup high-quality unsweetened cocoa powder
5 tablespoons cornstarch
1 quart whole milk
1 cup sugar
¼ teaspoon salt
2 ounces best-quality bittersweet chocolate, chopped
1½ teaspoons vanilla extract
1½ cups very cold heavy cream whipped together with
    3 tablespoons sugar and ½ teaspoon vanilla extract,
    for garnish
¼ cup shaved milk or dark chocolate, for garnish

1. Melt the butter in a medium saucepan.
2. Meanwhile, place the cocoa powder, cornstarch, milk,
sugar, and salt in a blender and blend for 1 minute.
3. Add the cocoa mixture to the melted butter, bring the
mixture to a boil, then lower the heat and simmer for
2 minutes, stirring constantly with a wire whisk (briskly
to ensure there are no lumps). Remove from the heat and
stir in the chopped chocolate. Continue to whisk another
minute to cool the mixture a bit, then whisk in the vanilla.
Rinse a 5- to 6-cup mold (see Note) with cold water.
Pour in the pudding mixture, smooth with a spatula, lay a
sheet of plastic wrap over the surface, and refrigerate
until cold (at least 6 hours and up to several days).
4. Run a sharp knife around the pudding and unmold it
onto a serving plate. If you have difficulty with this, dip
the mold very briefly in hot water or wrap it in a kitchen
towel that has been dipped in hot water.
5. Dollop or use a pastry bag to pipe whipped cream on
top of the pudding and then top with chocolate shavings.

Note: The pudding can also be divided among 6 to 8
smaller molds.

Red Wine Jelly

An English medieval feast traditionally included at least one jelly, usually combining both meat and fruit flavors. Not until Tudor times was a division made between the sweet and savory versions. Sweet jellies, often layered by color, were an important component of Tudor and Stuart "banquets," a word which, at the time, referred not to the feast itself but rather the often bizarre (by today's standards, at least) sweet course accompanied by entertainment. Pies opened to release the well-known four-and-twenty blackbirds or sometimes even frogs, which in the words of one seventeenth-century writer "made the ladies skip and shreek."

These brightly colored jellies were popular throughout much of fashionable Europe. Emphasizing color rather than flavor, they were used to create elaborate and decorative tablescapes depicting fish, flowers, and fruit in both landscape and still life tableaux. A glistening wine jelly on a pedestaled stand was often the centerpiece finale of a grand feast.

This Red Wine Jelly emphasizes both color and flavor. A grown-up dessert, it is tart and sophisticated due to the inclusion of red wine nicely rounded out by brandy. The whipped cream is a good counterpoint to the austerity of the jelly.

Serves 6

1 bottle Bordeaux or any good red wine
Grated zest and juice of 1 orange
Grated zest and juice of 1 lemon
6 tablespoons brandy
1 cup sugar
1 cup red currant jelly
4 tablespoons (4 packets) powdered gelatin
2 cups very cold heavy cream whipped together with
    2 tablespoons sugar

1. Stir the first 6 ingredients (everything except the gelatin and the whipped cream) together in a medium-sized saucepan.
2. Sprinkle the gelatin over the top and whisk in.
3. Bring to a boil and boil over medium heat for 5 minutes.
4. Pass the jelly through a sieve into a rinsed and damp 7- to 8-cup mold and refrigerate until cold and set, at least 4 hours.
5. Unmold and serve with the whipped cream.

Variation: A more delicate jelly can be made using less gelatin (3 packets), but then do not try to unmold it. Serve it straight from the mold. A heatproof glass bowl is beautiful if you serve the jelly at the table, passing the whipped cream separately.

Chocolate Bread Pudding

WITH BRANDY CUSTARD SAUCE

This dessert elevates a beloved comfort food to new heights. Already smooth, rich, creamy, and chocolatey, the addition of a subtle brandy crème anglaise makes this baked mélange of buttered brioche and chocolate custard sophisticated and elegant as well.

Though particularly good in late fall or winter, chocolate bread pudding was on Arcadia's menu year-round. It was the chosen autumn dessert in Anne Rosenzweig's *The Arcadia Seasonal Mural and Cookbook* (1986), but her customers demanded it no matter what the season. This signature dish was given rave reviews virtually every time the restaurant was mentioned in print. In the *New York Times* in 1985, Brian Miller wrote, "Miss Rosenzweig, who began her career as a pastry chef, makes the desserts, and they are sublime. Chocolate Bread Pudding with Brandy Custard Sauce has me seriously considering a move to East Sixty-second Street. The rectangle of spongy dark chocolate is rich, but not excessive, and the brandy custard is good enough to drink." Nine years later, in the same newspaper, Ruth Reichl wrote, "And who could resist that warm chocolate bread pudding? I had that bread pudding when the restaurant opened. I am delighted to find it still on the menu."

In her cookbook, Rosenzweig suggests serving the bread pudding after a fig, gorgonzola, walnut, and mixed-green salad, followed by a main course of roast quail, savoy cabbage, and kasha. The pudding would also be equally good after a simple roast chicken or pork loin, or baked salmon. Rosenzweig recommends serving this very rich dessert with a dark, sweet fortified wine such as a late-harvest California zinfandel, a Malmsey Madeira, a cream sherry, or a ruby port, although it can certainly stand very well on its own.

Be sure to use a high-quality dark chocolate (Callebaut or Valrhona are two good options), but whichever you use, on a chilly day in late fall or winter, make this dessert. Everyone who tastes it will be glad you did.

Serves 8 to 10

For the bread pudding:
1 (12-inch) loaf of brioche or egg bread, cut into
    12 slices
1 cup (2 sticks) unsalted butter, melted
½ pound best-quality bittersweet chocolate, chopped
3 cups heavy cream
1 cup whole milk
1 cup sugar
12 large egg yolks
1 teaspoon vanilla extract
Pinch of salt

For the brandy custard sauce:
3 large egg yolks
⅓ cup sugar
Pinch of salt
⅓ cup milk
1 cup heavy cream
¼ cup brandy

To make the bread pudding:
1. Preheat the oven to 425 degrees. Brush the bread slices with the melted butter and place them on a baking sheet. Toast in the oven, turning once, until golden brown. Watch carefully so they do not burn.
2. Melt the chocolate in the top of a double boiler or in a metal bowl set over a saucepan of simmering water.
3. Place the cream and the milk in a saucepan and bring almost to a boil. Meanwhile, whisk the sugar and egg yolks together in a large bowl until well blended. Slowly whisk in the hot cream mixture. Pour the mixture through a sieve into a bowl and skim off any foam. Add the melted chocolate, the vanilla, and salt and whisk until well combined.
4. Arrange the toasted bread in two overlapping rows in a 9-by-12-inch baking dish. Pour the chocolate mixture

over, cover with plastic wrap, and place a smaller pan on top to keep the bread submerged in the sauce. Add weights such as canned food or small dishes, if needed.
5. Let stand for at least one hour until the bread is soaked through. Remove the weights, smaller pan, and plastic wrap. Preheat the oven to 325 degrees.
6. Put the baking dish in a bain marie (a larger pan with hot water that comes halfway up the sides of the baking dish) and bake until the liquid has been absorbed and the pudding is almost set in the center, about 1 hour and 45 minutes.
Note: If you want to experiment, banana slices tucked between the pieces of bread before baking produce a delicious result.

To make the brandy custard sauce:
1. In a medium-sized bowl, beat the egg yolks together with the sugar and salt until well blended.
2. In a saucepan, bring the milk and cream just to a boil. Slowly add the hot liquid to the egg yolk mixture, stirring constantly.
3. Return the custard mixture to the saucepan and cook over medium-low heat, stirring constantly, until it thickens enough to coat the back of the spoon. Do not boil.
4. Remove from the heat and cool to lukewarm. Then add the brandy and pour through a sieve into a bowl; let cool to room temperature, then chill. Serve cold in a pitcher accompanying the bread pudding.

Variation: Quadruple the sauce recipe and use the sauce instead of the chocolate custard to make a vanilla-brandy bread pudding (add 2 teaspoons vanilla extract along with the brandy). This version is particularly good if you soak dried apricots and prunes in the brandy for a couple of hours ahead of time, then tuck the soaked fruits in among the bread slices and use the remaining brandy (topped up if necessary) for the pudding mixture.

PIES, TORTES, and FRUITS

Edna Lewis's Peach Cobbler with Nutmeg Sauce

Arcadia's Pear and Ginger Crumble
with Lemon Curd Ice Cream

Marjorie Kinnan Rawlings's Black Bottom Pie

Miss Grimble's Chocolate Angel Pie

Seidel Torte

Ultra Violet's Chocolate and Chestnut Torte

Melon Surprise

Frédy Girardet's Tarte au Raisiné

La Pyramide's Pruneaux au Pichet

Apple Charlotte

Michael Field's Chocolate Torrone Loaf

EDNA LEWIS'S

Peach Cobbler

WITH NUTMEG SAUCE

Culinary icon Edna Lewis was born in 1916 in Freetown, Virginia, a tiny settlement of farm buildings founded by three emancipated slaves, one of them her grandfather. For the Freetown community, growing, gathering, and preparing food was a way of life. Lewis became a devotee of seasonal eating, farm-fresh, natural ingredients, and home-style country cooking. She received award after award for her dedication to "educating a nation about the nuances of Southern cooking." Lewis put an end to the "knee-slapping cornpone image of Southern food among many American cooks," noted Eric Asimov and Kim Severson in the 2006 obituary they wrote for her in the *New York Times*. In 1999 she was named a Grande Dame by Les Dames d'Escoffier, an honor which Lewis saw as her crowning achievement. She had become a chef to be reckoned with in America at a time when female chefs, let alone black ones, were a rarity.

In describing Lewis's *The Taste of Country Cooking,* a reviewer states, "The rhythm of farm work and holiday feast follows the back-and-forth between people and nature, revealing a regional cuisine's original connection to the soil. Lewis's advocacy of natural foods reflects not the zeal of a convert but the living memory of being a farm girl in Freetown, where the woods and orchard and garden were her supermarket." In a 1989 *New York Times* interview, Lewis said, "As a child in Virginia, I thought all food tasted delicious. After growing up, I didn't think food tasted the same, so it has been my lifelong effort to try and recapture those good flavors of the past."

In 1949 she opened Cafe Nicholson in Manhattan with antiques dealer John Nicholson. The restaurant soon became a hangout for artists, bohemians, and fashionistas; regulars included Diana Vreeland, Richard Avedon, and fellow southerners Truman Capote and Tennessee Williams. Her last important restaurant stint began in 1988, when at age seventy-two she was hired to head the kitchen at Brooklyn's Gage & Tollner. With her cornbread, catfish, she-crab soup, and deep-dish pies and cobblers, Lewis turned the failing restaurant around, and it remained a beloved Brooklyn institution until it closed in 2004. She mingled old and new in a way that went on to influence a generation of new American chefs: Jeremiah Tower, Wolfgang Puck, Alice Waters, Jonathan Waxman, and Jaspar White, to name a few.

This Peach Cobbler is quintessential Edna Lewis in all its Southern-summer deliciousness. The Nutmeg Sauce provides an unusual and appropriately old-fashioned accompaniment. I adapted the cobbler (mine has less sugar and less butter) from her book *The Taste of Country Cooking*. The recipe also appears in a slightly different form in *In Pursuit of Flavor*, where she remembers, "With the first juicy, sweet peaches of summer, we always made cobbler." For Lewis, the whole point of this dessert is to taste sweet, fresh peaches—nothing else. She suggests using the sweetest fruit you can find and recommends the Nutmeg Sauce, but admits that growing up, "we would just spoon the juice from the peaches up over the cobbler which is good too."

The cobbler is well-matched with vanilla ice cream à la mode, as recommended in *The Joy of Cooking*, which describes cobblers as "simply deep-dish single-crusted fruit pies," with the crust "usually on the top, though occasionally . . . on the bottom." It goes on to state, "Cobblers used to be made with pie dough, but a sweet rich biscuit dough is more common today." Lewis's pie-dough cobbler has the unusual aspect of both a bottom *and* a top crust, its slightly salty crunch intensifying the peach flavor even further. Introducing her recipe, Lewis notes, "In Virginia it is traditional to weave a lattice top pastry over the fruit, which is piled generously into a deep pie plate and mounded a little in the center."

Serves 6 to 8

Butter Pie Pastry (recipe follows), lightly chilled
8 large ripe but still firm peaches (or substitute nectarines)
¾ cup sugar mixed with a large pinch of salt
4 tablespoons (½ stick) cold unsalted butter cut into thin slices
Nutmeg Sauce (recipe follows)

1. Lightly butter an 8-inch square baking dish.
2. Divide the pastry disk in half. Roll one half between two sheets of wax or parchment paper to fit in the baking dish; line the pan with the dough, pressing it gently into the sides, bottom, and corners of the pan. Trim the overlapping dough from around the edges. Refrigerate the lined pan until ready to use, at least 30 minutes. Several hours or overnight will provide an even more tender crust.
3. Roll out the other piece of dough into a 9-inch square; cut twelve 9-inch strips, each about ¾ inch wide. Place the strips between wax paper and refrigerate them.
4. Preheat the oven to 450 degrees.
5. Peel the peaches (peeling is unnecessary if using nectarines) with a vegetable peeler or by dipping each one in boiling water for 20 to 60 seconds, refreshing in cold water, then slipping the skin off. Remove the pit and slice each peach into 8 wedges.
6. Sprinkle 2 tablespoons of the sugar-salt mixture over the dough in the pan. Mound the peaches in the middle. Sprinkle all but 1 tablespoon of the remaining sugar mixture over them and distribute the butter slices evenly over the top.
7. Weave the pastry strips into a lattice by placing one lengthwise and then one crosswise, spacing them evenly, until they are all used. Moisten the ends of the strips with cold water and press them into the crust sides to seal. Don't worry if they break. Just patch them back together as best you can.
8. Sprinkle the remaining 1 tablespoon sugar mixture over the lattice.
9. Place the baking dish in the middle of the preheated oven, and immediately lower the oven temperature to 425. Bake until the crust is deep golden and the fruit juices are bubbling, about 45 minutes. Let cool for at least 30 minutes before serving with the Nutmeg Sauce, if desired.

Note: Miss Lewis's cobbler is quite runny. You'll need a spoon to scoop up all of the delicious juices. If you want a "fork only" version, toss a tablespoon of cornstarch or 2 tablespoons of instant tapioca with the fruit before placing it in the crust.

BUTTER PIE PASTRY

Makes enough for 1 (8-inch)
double-crust cobbler

3 cups unbleached all-purpose flour
$1\frac{1}{4}$ teaspoons salt
18 tablespoons (2 sticks plus 2 tablespoons) very cold
   unsalted butter cut into small pieces

1. Put the flour and salt in a food processor and pulse to combine.
2. Add the butter and pulse until the mixture is the texture of very coarse cornmeal.
3. With the motor running, add $\frac{3}{8}$ cup ice water all at once and pulse just until combined. If too dry to come together, pulse in another 1 to 3 teaspoons of ice water. The dough should not become a solid mass. (This can also be done with a pastry blender, two knives, or your fingers, but I find the food processor method much easier.)
4. Form the dough into a ball with your hands. Dust with flour and flatten into a disk. Wrap in plastic and refrigerate for at least 30 minutes.

NUTMEG SAUCE

Makes about $1\frac{1}{2}$ cups

$\frac{2}{3}$ cup sugar
Pinch of salt
2 teaspoons cornstarch
$\frac{1}{4}$ teaspoon freshly grated nutmeg
1 cup boiling water
1 2-inch piece dried orange peel (see Note), 1 teaspoon
   finely grated orange zest, or $\frac{1}{8}$ teaspoon orange oil
3 tablespoons brandy
1 tablespoon heavy cream (optional)

1. Mix the sugar, salt, cornstarch, and nutmeg together in a small saucepan.
2. Whisk in the boiling water, add the orange peel, zest, or oil and simmer over low heat for 10 minutes, whisking occasionally.
3. Let cool for 5 minutes, then stir in the brandy.
4. Reheat before serving, adding the optional cream; do not boil.

Note: To dry orange peel, scrape away and discard all the white pith from pieces of peel. Dry the scraped peel on a rack for several days. Store for up to 1 month in a lidded jar.

Pear and Ginger Crumble

WITH LEMON CURD ICE CREAM

When I was in cooking school, the pastry chef from New York's famed restaurant Arcadia (see page 25) came to class and showed us how to make her scrumptious crumbles. This recipe is my adaptation of what she made that day. Pears and ginger are a perfect combination; if you choose to include the optional candied ginger in addition to the ground, so much the better. Its unexpected chewiness lends an interesting contrast to the softness of the fruit and slight crunchiness of the topping. The warm crumble is delicious paired with the rich and silky Lemon Curd Ice Cream. You can also experiment with other fruits: like the pears, apples are good in fall and winter, just replace the ginger with raisins plumped in rum, brandy, or Calvados; in summer, use stone fruits or berries, and add toasted and ground almonds to the topping. Grated lemon zest is nice mixed into the fruit. If the stone fruits or berries are particularly juicy, toss them with a couple of tablespoons of flour or instant tapioca before filling the ramekins.

The crumbles can be prepared through step 4 up to twenty-four hours ahead. Refrigerate, and then pop them into the oven as you sit down to dinner (be sure to bring them to room temperature before baking). They will bake and then cool to a perfect lukewarm just in time for dessert. Or bake them in the afternoon and warm them briefly in the oven when ready to serve. In summer, the lemon curd itself is the perfect filling for a tart or lemon meringue pie, or use it to fill meringue shells garnished with fresh blueberries and a scoop of vanilla ice cream.

Serves 6

About 4 tablespoons (½ stick) unsalted butter, softened
   to grease the molds
¼ cup brown sugar
Pinch of salt
¼ teaspoon ground cinnamon
⅛ teaspoon freshly grated nutmeg
2 teaspoons ground ginger or fresh ginger put though
   a garlic press

Finely grated zest of one lemon
¼ cup finely diced crystallized ginger (optional)
6 ripe Anjou pears, peeled, cored, and cut into
   bite-sized pieces
1 tablespoon all-purpose flour or instant tapioca,
   if needed
Crumble Topping (recipe follows)
Lemon Curd Ice Cream (recipe follows)

1. Preheat the oven to 350 degrees. Generously butter six ¾- or 1-cup ramekins or charlotte molds.

2. In a large bowl, combine the brown sugar, salt, cinnamon, nutmeg, ground or fresh ginger, lemon zest, and crystallized ginger, if using. Add the pears and toss to combine. If the pears are very juicy, add the flour or instant tapioca and toss to combine.

3. Divide the fruit mixture evenly among the prepared ramekins.

4. Divide the Crumble Topping into 6 portions. For each fruit-filled ramekin, take a portion of crumble and sprinkle it over the pear mixture. Cover the fruit completely, leaving no fruit showing. Use all of the topping.

5. Place the ramekins on a baking sheet and bake for 30 to 35 minutes, until the crumble is just beginning to color.

6. Serve immediately or reheat in the lower third of a 450-degree oven. Place each ramekin on a dessert plate and serve with a scoop of Lemon Curd Ice Cream on top.

Note: Do not use Bartlett pears; they are too juicy. Boscs are fine, but they will take longer to cook.

CRUMBLE TOPPING

¾ cup (1½ sticks) unsalted butter, at room temperature
1½ cups light brown sugar
1⅓ cups all-purpose flour
1½ teaspoons ground cinnamon
⅛ teaspoon freshly grated nutmeg
Pinch of salt

1. In a medium-sized bowl, mix the butter and the brown sugar until just combined, not soft and creamy.

2. Sift the flour together with the cinnamon, nutmeg, and salt. Add to the butter mixture, stirring until completely blended but still crumbly.

LEMON CURD ICE CREAM

Makes 2 quarts

2 large eggs, plus 2 yolks
½ cup plus 1 tablespoon sugar
Pinch of salt
1 heaping tablespoon finely grated lemon zest, plus finely grated zest of 2 lemons
7 tablespoons fresh lemon juice
9 tablespoons unsalted butter, chilled and cut into little pieces
3 cups very cold Crème Anglaise (page 190)

1. Whisk together the eggs, egg yolks, sugar, salt, 1 tablespoon lemon zest, and lemon juice in a medium-sized heavy-bottomed saucepan.

2. Cook over medium heat, stirring constantly while adding the butter pieces a few at a time.

3. Keep stirring until the mixture is quite thick, but do not let it come to a simmer.

4. Remove from the heat and immediately pour into a ceramic or nonreactive metal bowl; you will have 2 cups of lemon curd. Lay plastic wrap directly on the lemon curd surface to prevent a skin from forming, poking a few holes in the plastic to release the steam. Let cool, then chill in the refrigerator until the lemon curd is very cold. The lemon curd can be made to this point 5 days in advance and refrigerated or frozen up to 3 months (see Note).

5. Mix the lemon curd with the cold crème anglaise and the lemon zest from two lemons and freeze in an ice cream maker according to manufacturer's instructions.

Note: Everything but the fruit can be prepared months in advance. The crumble topping can be refrigerated for up to a month and frozen for several. The lemon curd keeps in the freezer for months, as does the crème anglaise; defrost to make the lemon curd ice cream.

MARJORIE KINNAN RAWLINGS'S

Black Bottom Pie

Marjorie Kinnan Rawlings, the Pulitzer Prize–winning author of *The Yearling*, gives this recipe for Black Bottom Pie in her 1942 bible of Southern gastronomy, *Cross Creek Cookery*. She calls it "the most delicious pie I have ever eaten." The unique combination of a gingersnap crust, separate layers of rich chocolate and rum custards, and an extravagant topping of whipped cream and chocolate shavings is definitely food for the gods. The recipe here deviates only slightly from the original. First of all, I double the amount of rum. As rumminess is a matter of personal preference, add the smaller amount, taste, and then add more if you see fit. And the number of gingersnaps in the crust is doubled. Some black bottom pies are made with a basic piecrust and some use chocolate cookies instead of gingersnaps; but for me, the crunchy, spicy ginger layer paired with the creamy custards is the whole raison d'être of this special pie. One final change: substitute heavy cream for Rawlings's "Dora's cream." (Dora was the author's Jersey cow.)

Serves 8

For the crust:
30 crisp (gingersnap-type) ginger cookies, store-bought or
    homemade (recipe follows)
5 tablespoons unsalted butter, melted

For the filling:
1 scant tablespoon (1 packet) powdered gelatin
1 cup sugar
1 tablespoon cornstarch
Pinch of salt
1¾ cups whole milk

4 large eggs, separated; yolks lightly beaten, whites
    reserved at room temperature
2½ ounces unsweetened chocolate, chopped
1 teaspoon vanilla extract
⅛ teaspoon cream of tartar
1 tablespoon dark rum, or a bit more to taste

For the topping:
1 cup very cold heavy cream
2 tablespoons confectioners' or superfine sugar
⅓ cup shaved bittersweet chocolate

To make the crust:

1. Preheat the oven to 350 degrees.
2. Pulse the gingersnaps in a food processor. Add the melted butter and process until combined. (Or crush the cookies with a rolling pin. Place in a bowl and then stir in the melted butter.)
3. Line a 9-inch pie pan, sides and bottom, with the crumb mixture. Press down hard. Bake for 10 minutes, and let cool.

To make the filling:

1. Stir the gelatin into ¼ cup cold water and set aside.
2. Combine ½ cup of the sugar with the cornstarch and the salt; set aside.
3. In a medium-sized saucepan, scald the milk, then stir in the sugar mixture and then the lightly beaten egg yolks. Cook over medium heat, stirring constantly, until the custard is quite thick, about 5 minutes. Stir in the dissolved gelatin. Transfer half of the custard to a bowl and set aside to cool.
4. In the top of a double boiler or in a metal bowl set over a saucepan of simmering water, melt the chocolate, then stir it into the custard in the saucepan. Stir in the vanilla. Spread this hot chocolate custard evenly over the bottom of the cooled crust. Refrigerate.
5. When the remaining custard is cool, use an electric mixer fitted with the whisk attachment to beat the egg whites together with the cream of tartar and a pinch of salt until very soft peaks form. Very gradually stir in the remaining ½ cup sugar so as not to deflate the egg whites. Fold the egg whites and rum into the cooled custard.
6. Spread the rum custard over the chocolate layer and refrigerate until set, about 4 to 6 hours or overnight.

To make the topping:

1. When ready to serve, whip the cream together with the sugar until soft peaks form. Spread the whipped cream over the pie. Sprinkle the shaved chocolate over the top. Serve cold.

Note: This recipe uses raw egg whites. If you are concerned about bacteria, or if serving to the young, elderly, or those with health issues, use pasteurized egg whites or liquid egg whites as a substitute. Also, there's less risk of bacteria with organic eggs.

GINGERSNAP COOKIES

Makes about 3 dozen 2-inch cookies

2 cups minus 2 tablespoons all-purpose flour
¾ teaspoon baking powder
¼ teaspoon baking soda
2½ teaspoons ground ginger
½ teaspoon ground cinnamon
1 large pinch ground cloves
⅛ teaspoon salt
6 tablespoons unsalted butter, at room temperature
¾ cup plus 4 teaspoons sugar
1 large egg, at room temperature
¼ cup dark molasses
¼ teaspoon finely grated lemon or orange zest
1 teaspoon freshly squeezed lemon juice

1. Preheat the oven to 350 degrees.
2. Sift together the first 7 ingredients and set aside.
3. Using an electric mixer, cream the butter and sugar until light and fluffy.
4. Add the egg, molasses, zest, and lemon juice and beat 5 minutes more.
5. Add the dry ingredients and mix just until combined.
6. With floured hands, pinch off small pieces of dough and roll them into one inch balls. Place the balls about 1½ inches apart on buttered or parchment-lined baking sheets. Pat the tops down to flatten slightly.
7. Bake on the upper rack of the oven for about 13 minutes or until the cookies are lightly browned and have begun to crack.
8. Transfer cookies to a rack to cool.
9. Store cooled cookies in an airtight container for up to a week. Freeze for longer storage.

Chocolate Angel Pie

Miss Grimble's was a beloved New York City institution in the 1960s and 1970s. *Town and Country* magazine raved about it, stating, "The chocolate cakes are chocolatier, the cheesecakes are creamier, the pecan pies are crunchier than most other places in New York."

"Angel" pies are defined by their meringue crust. This one has a chocolate-Kahlúa filling and is topped with whipped cream, strawberries, and an abundance of shaved chocolate. I love meringue and am in complete agreement with Sylvia Balser Hirsch, aka Miss Grimble, who said this about her pie: "Desserts are my business, and I find this possibly the most irresistible one in all dessertdom. Dieters fall off their diets and strong men go weak at the sight of it. It is beautiful to behold and luscious to eat." This recipe is adapted from Hirsch's 1983 cookbook *Miss Grimble Presents Delicious Desserts*, in which she decorated the pie with strawberries. You can use raspberries instead, and sometimes, especially in winter, it is chic to serve it sprinkled with a few chocolate-covered coffee beans, or ungarnished altogether.

Serves *8*

For the meringue crust:
4 large eggs, separated, whites at room temperature
    (refrigerate the yolks and reserve for the filling)
Large pinch of salt
¼ teaspoon cream of tartar
1 cup plus 2 tablespoons sugar
½ teaspoon vanilla extract

For the filling:
12 ounces semisweet chocolate, chopped
5 teaspoons instant espresso powder, such as
    Medaglia D'Oro

Pinch of salt
4 large egg yolks (reserved from meringue crust)
1 cup very cold heavy cream
2 tablespoons Kahlúa

For the topping:
1 cup very cold heavy cream
¼ cup sugar (superfine is preferable)
1 teaspoon vanilla extract
1 pint fresh strawberries, hulled and sliced, or
    fresh raspberries (optional)
⅓ cup shaved semisweet chocolate (optional)

To make the meringue crust:

1. Preheat the oven to 275 degrees. Lightly butter a 9-inch springform pan or a pie pan with a removable bottom and line the bottom with parchment paper; butter the paper.
2. Using an electric mixer fitted with the whisk attachment, beat the egg whites together with the salt on low speed until foamy. Add the cream of tartar and continue beating. When the whites are opaque and beginning to stiffen, increase the speed to medium and begin adding the sugar. Beating constantly, continue to add it very slowly so as not to deflate the egg whites. When all the sugar has been added, add the vanilla and increase the speed to high. Continue beating until the egg whites are very stiff.
3. Spread the meringue mixture evenly over the bottom and up the sides of the prepared pan, building up the sides about 2 inches (enough to hold the filling).
4. Place the pie pan on a baking sheet and bake for 1 hour and 15 minutes. Remove from the oven and let cool.

To make the filling:

1. Place the chocolate, instant espresso powder, salt, and ¾ cup water in the top of a double boiler or in a metal bowl set over a saucepan of simmering water. Heat until the chocolate has just melted, stirring frequently.
2. Remove from the heat and beat in the egg yolks, one at a time. Let the mixture cool completely.
3. Whip the cream until soft peaks form. Beat in the Kahlúa, then fold the mixture into the completely cooled chocolate. Refrigerate.

To assemble the pie and make the topping:

1. Spoon the chocolate filling into the meringue shell, smooth the top and refrigerate until set, for at least 4 hours. The pie can be refrigerated for up to 24 hours at this point.
2. When ready to serve, carefully remove the pie from the pan and place it on a serving platter.
3. Whip the 1 cup cream together with the sugar and vanilla until fairly stiff. Spread the whipped cream over the chocolate filling and decorate with the berries. Sprinkle with the shaved chocolate and serve.

Seidel Torte

E asy to make and delightfully foolproof, Seidel Torte is a dessert in the tradition of linzer and sacher tortes, but unusual in its use of red currant jam and in the addition of brandy to the pastry. Hanni Nyffeler Nussbaumer made her Seidel Torte six times a year every year throughout her entire adult life. This was her family's favorite cake, and all six of Nussbaumer's children, three sons and three daughters, requested it for their birthdays every year. She learned to make the Seidel Torte at culinary school in her native Switzerland before moving as a young bride to Oak Grove, Kentucky, in 1930. It was the only birthday cake her family ever made. When Nussbaumer's daughters reached their teens and learned to cook, they continued the tradition, making it for their parents' birthdays also; quite a bit of Seidel Torte, but no one complained.

Heidi Hough, one of Nussbaumer's three daughters, gave me this recipe. Hough describes growing up on the family's dairy farm sixty miles north of Nashville, on the Kentucky-Tennessee state line. The farm was completely self-sufficient. Mr. Nussbaumer even made the family's bread using his own stone-ground flour, as he found the store-bought variety "too doughy." Mrs. Nussbaumer took advantage of the farm's perfect ingredients to create restaurant–style European food for her family. Cooking with spirits, whipping up a soufflé at a moment's notice, and making a wine or hollandaise sauce were all commonplace in her kitchen, though these activities initially raised eyebrows in the community. There were no other "foreigners" in that part of the state, and the Nussbaumers were well known. Homesick Europeans visiting the area often made a pilgrimage to the dairy farm to speak their native languages and eat food they found familiar—basically to savor a taste of home.

Serves 6

1⅔ cups toasted, blanched almonds (hazelnuts can be
    substituted)
1 cup plus 2 tablespoons sugar
Finely grated zest of 1 lemon
Large pinch of salt
1 cup (2 sticks) unsalted butter, at room temperature
1 large egg
1 tablespoon brandy
1½ cups all-purpose flour
2 cups red currant jam or preserves (not jelly),
    or raspberry, apricot, or another flavor of jam
1 large egg yolk, beaten

1. Preheat the oven to 350 degrees. Line the bottom of a 10-inch springform pan with parchment paper.
2. Put the almonds and sugar in a food processor and pulse until very finely ground. Add the lemon zest and salt, then add the butter and pulse several times to cut it in.
3. Pulse in the egg and brandy, then the flour. Do not overwork, but be sure the ingredients are thoroughly combined.
4. Divide the dough into two parts that are almost equal. Press the larger part evenly into the bottom of the lined pan and bake until the edges are slightly brown, about 20 minutes. Remove from the oven and let cool completely on a wire rack.
5. Roll some of the reserved dough into several short cylinders about ⅜-inch in diameter. Make a border by piecing them together around the edge of the baked dough. (If the dough is too soft, refrigerate it briefly.)
6. Fill with the jam.
7. Roll out the remaining dough between two pieces of wax paper and place in the freezer or refrigerator to harden slightly. If too hard, the dough will be brittle and break. Cut into ½-inch strips and make a lattice on top of the jam, attaching the ends of the strips to the dough border.
8. Brush the dough border and the lattice with the egg yolk and bake until golden, 25 to 35 minutes. Let cool, then serve warm at room temperature.

Note: This torte freezes well. Let it thaw and then heat it for a few minutes in a 350-degree oven before serving. Hough insists it is much better warm, though it is also very good at room temperature.

Chocolate and Chestnut Torte

"I made this cake in 1970 for Easter, as Warhol was coming to visit me in my Tower apartment above the Guggenheim Museum. After lunch, the two of us ate the whole cake and felt as satisfied as robins in love.

Andy said to me: 'That cake tops all the others, it is a 5 star winner.' He called me the next day begging for more. 'I am addicted. Luckily it is a legal drug. My pupils are still dilated, just to think of it.' The cake became a ritual, an easy secret rendezvous as we lived only three blocks apart. Our love affair was chocolate."

So reminisces Isabelle Collin Dufresne, aka Ultra Violet, about her Chocolate and Chestnut Torte. The dessert is the platonic essence of those two ingredients, as it contains nothing else other than a few tablespoons of heavy cream.

Ultra Violet grew up rich, beautiful, and convent-educated in Grenoble, France, where she first came across this very French dessert. She later rebelled against school, the nuns, and her haute-bourgeois family and fled to New York City. She met and became the muse of Salvador Dalí and soon knew everyone from Marcel Duchamp to Man Ray, Howard Hughes, and Richard Nixon, but she is best known for her involvement with Warhol's Factory starting in the early 1960s. She was his first "superstar" and played roles in a number of his films including *The Life of Juanita Castro* (1965), ****(1966), and *I, A Man* (1967). She left the Factory in the late 1960s to concentrate on her own artwork.

This unique torte is a chocolate lover's fantasy enhanced by the subtle presence of chestnut. Whether you cover the torte with the Chocolate Glaze and decorate it with a pure gold leaf as Ultra suggests, or pile it with a mountain of the Crème Fouettée as Eduard de Pomiane recommends when giving a similar recipe in his book, *Cooking with Pomiane,* or do both, it is mysterious and sophisticated, and not too sweet. If you decide to do nothing but dust it with a bit of powdered sugar just before serving, it's a snap to make—now that you can easily find high-quality peeled frozen chestnuts in fancy gourmet food shops.

Serves 8 to 12

1 pound fresh, frozen, or vacuum-packed peeled chestnuts
1⁄8 teaspoon salt
1⁄2 cup heavy cream
12 ounces semisweet or bittersweet chocolate, chopped
    into small pieces
Crème Fouettée (recipe follows)
Shaved semisweet chocolate or Chocolate Glaze
    (recipe follows) and one gold leaf (very optional)

1. Put the chestnuts in a medium-sized saucepan and cover with cool water by about 2 inches. Add the salt and bring to a boil. Immediately lower the heat, cover the pan, and simmer until the chestnuts are very tender, about 20 minutes. Check tenderness with the point of a knife.
2. Drain the chestnuts and pat them dry with a tea towel. Pass the chestnuts through a potato ricer twice or push them through a sieve, then stir in the cream.
3. Meanwhile, melt the chopped chocolate in the top of a double boiler or in a metal bowl set over a saucepan of simmering water. Add the melted chocolate to the chestnut mixture. Stir until combined. If the mixture gets too cool to stir, place the bowl over simmering water and stir until tepid and pliable.
4. Butter an 8- to 9-inch loaf pan and line the bottom with wax or parchment paper, or aluminum foil. While still warm, transfer the chestnut mixture to the prepared pan. Refrigerate, covered, for at least 5 hours and up to 2 days. When ready to serve, run a sharp knife around the edge and invert onto a serving plate. Serve topped with Crème Fouettée or lightly sweetened whipped cream and shaved chocolate, or, as Ultra Violet suggests, with a chocolate glaze with a real gold leaf placed in the center.

CRÈME FOUETTÉE

2 large egg whites, at room temperature
Pinch of salt
3⁄4 cup cold heavy cream
2 to 3 tablespoons milk
1⁄2 teaspoons vanilla extract
1 tablespoon confectioners' sugar, sifted

1. Using an electric mixer fitted with the whisk attachment, beat the egg whites and salt until soft peaks form. Set aside.
2. Place the cream, milk, vanilla, and confectioners' sugar in a separate bowl and beat until soft peaks form.
3. Fold the egg whites into the cream mixture and refrigerate, covered, until ready to use (no more than 3 hours).

Note: This recipe uses raw egg whites. If you are concerned about bacteria, or if serving to the young, elderly, or those with health issues, use pasteurized egg whites or liquid egg whites as a substitute. Also, there's less risk of bacteria with organic eggs.

CHOCOLATE GLAZE

2 ounces semisweet or bittersweet chocolate, cut into
    small pieces
1 1⁄2 ounces unsweetened chocolate, cut into small pieces
1 1⁄2 teaspoons tasteless vegetable oil such as canola

1. Place all the ingredients in the top of a double boiler or in a metal bowl set over a saucepan of simmering water. Heat, stirring occasionally, until the chocolate is almost melted. Remove from the heat and stir until completely melted.
2. Place the cake on a wire rack and put a plate or piece of wax paper under the rack to catch the extra glaze. Pour the glaze onto the cake and use a metal spatula to spread it evenly over the top and around the sides of the cake. If using, place a gold leaf in the center of the cake. Let the glaze harden for at least 2 hours before serving.

Melon Surprise

My mother taught me two tricks with melon: one very simple and one much more elaborate. The simple trick was to sprinkle salt and lime juice on fresh cantaloupe. The more complicated endeavor was something she called "piñata melon," and was my favorite summer dessert as a child. (The name refers to the candy-filled Mexican papier-mâché piñatas.)

My mother cut a hole in the top of a melon, emptied the interior of seeds, and spooned out the flesh. She then combined the flesh with sugar, fresh orange juice, and a variety of berries and cut-up summer fruit. This mixture was returned to the melon, as was the melon's top. The next day (after refrigerating the whole thing overnight), reminiscent of a piñata we cut into the melon and were greeted by the colorful bounty of California "high summer." For adult dinner guests Champagne was added to the mix and it was then called melon en surprise, but I was quite happy eating it à la piñata.

Only in researching this book did I learn that my mother did not invent this dessert; rather, its origins go back centuries to a time when a liquor-filled melon was cooled overnight in a well before gracing an elegant summer picnic—perhaps in Paris's Bois de Boulogne or at a mid-August garden-party at Sissinghurst Castle. Although I was a bit disappointed in my mother's lack of originality, I was thrilled with the romance of this newfound history.

Over the centuries this melon-surprise idea has taken many forms. Sometimes the melon is seeded and filled with liquor—port, Champagne, Kirsch, or Sauternes. Often, as in my mother's version, the flesh is scooped out and made into a fruit salad; in other versions, the flesh is left in place. Sometimes the melon is dyed a beautiful color; other times it remains *au nature*, depending on the type of liquor and the fruit used. Photographer Eric Boman remembers the melons of his Swedish childhood turning a beautiful purple when filled with blueberries and vodka.

This dessert is best when made with as many types of fruits and berries as possible. Local greenmarkets can be treasure troves of fabulous fruit, including hard-to-find varieties such as red currants; sour and sweet cherries; tiny apricots; green, red, and sugar plums; and gooseberries.

Serves 4 to 10 (depending on melon size)

1 melon such as a cantaloupe, cranshaw, musk melon, orange-fleshed honeydew, or cavaillon. Make sure the melon is attractive and can stand up (balance) on a platter if you want the drama of cutting it at the table.

A mixture of some or all of the following: Blueberries, raspberries, slices of strawberries, fresh currants; thinly sliced peeled peaches and apricots; thinly sliced nectarines and plums; halved grapes; cherries; watermelon, honeydew, and/or other melon cut into ¾-inch dice

¼ cup (or more depending on size of melon) freshly squeezed orange juice

½ cup (or more) Champagne, Grand Marnier, Madeira, Lillet, port, or Sauternes

Pinch of salt

Sugar to taste (1 to 3 tablespoons, depending on size of melon and sweetness desired)

1. Using a thin, sharp knife, cut a round plug out of the top of the melon (similar to what you do when carving a pumpkin). Use a large spoon to remove all the seeds.
2. In a large bowl, mix the fruit with the juice and the liquor. Stir in salt and the sugar to taste.
3. Fill the melon with this mixture and replace the plug. Refrigerate for 12 to 24 hours.
4. When ready to serve, stand the melon on a large platter (if it will not balance, cut a sliver off the bottom to create a flat surface). Slice it at the table as the presentation is a major factor. Each portion should have a slice of melon and some of the macerated fruit.

FRÉDY GIRARDET'S

Tarte au Raisiné

In 1976 the *New York Times* called the Swiss perfectionist Frédy Girardet "the World's Greatest New Chef." He was considered by many to be the most important chef of the twentieth century. Joel Robuchon declared he was "*le meilleur des meilleur chefs de la planète*." Girardet is known for his quiet, meticulous manner, and his integrity, which informs everything he does. The understated perfection of his food reflects the character of the man.

After inheriting his father's bistro, located in the Old Town Hall in Crissier, a suburb of Lausanne, Switzerland, he renamed it and turned Frédy Girardet into a three-star Michelin establishment, and arguably the best restaurant in the world, a reputation maintained until he sold it in 1996.

This tart is Girardet's version of an old country recipe from the Vaud, the region in southwest Switzerland where his restaurant was located. Local farmers boil down a mixture of apple and pear juices to make *raisiné*, the thick, fruity concentrate that is the basis of this delicious and unusual tart. Use imported raisiné if you can find it, but Girardet's reasonable facsimile yields excellent results.

Serves 6

For the tart shell:
2 cups all-purpose flour
¼ cup sugar
½ teaspoon salt
1 cup (2 sticks) very cold unsalted butter

For the filling:
1 cup fresh, unfiltered apple or pear juice, or a mixture
Small piece of orange zest
Pinch of ground cloves
Pinch of ground cinnamon
3 large eggs, plus 1 yolk
½ cup heavy cream

To make the tart shell:
1. Thoroughly combine the flour, sugar, and salt.
2. Cut the butter into 1-inch cubes, toss with the dry ingredients, and refrigerate or freeze for 5 to 10 minutes.
3. Place the flour-butter mixture in the bowl of a food processor and pulse about 15 times, until the butter particles are the size of small peas. With the motor running, add ¼ cup ice water all at once through the feed tube and process for about 10 seconds, stopping the machine before the dough becomes a solid mass. Form the dough into a ball and then a disk. Refrigerate the dough if it is too sticky.
4. Butter an 8-inch tart pan with a removable bottom and fluted edge.
5. Using a rolling pin, roll the dough into a circle about 13 inches in diameter (placing the dough between 2 pieces of wax paper makes this easier). The rolled dough should be about ⅛ to ³⁄₁₆ inch thick. Fit the rolled dough into the prepared pan. Cut off the extra dough and crimp the edges. Prick the tart shell bottom all over with a fork. Refrigerate for a least 1 hour, and preferably several hours or overnight, to tenderize the crust and help prevent shrinkage. Any extra dough can be frozen for future use.
6. Preheat the oven to 350 degrees. Line the tart shell with aluminum foil and dried beans or pie weights and place on a baking sheet. Bake in the lower third of the oven until just set and no longer shiny (peak under the foil to ascertain this), about 15 minutes.
7. Remove the beans or weights and foil. Lower the oven temperate to 300 degrees and continue baking until the crust is light gold, 10 to 15 minutes more. The tart shell can be baked up to 2 days ahead or used immediately while still hot.

To make the filling:
1. In a small saucepan over low heat, make the raisiné by cooking the apple and/or pear juice, orange zest, and spices until reduced to ⅓ cup. Set aside to cool.
2. Preheat the oven to 350 degrees.
3. Whisk together the eggs, egg yolk, cream, and raisiné.
4. Place the tart shell in its pan on a baking sheet and add the filling; fill to the top.
5. Place in the oven and bake with the oven door slightly ajar until the filling is wobbly in the center but no longer liquid when you shake the pan, about 20 to 25 minutes.
6. Let cool on a wire rack for 45 minutes and remove from the pan when almost cool. Finish cooling the tart on the rack.

Pruneaux au Pichet

(PRUNES IN A PITCHER)

In *Blue Trout and Black Truffles* (1953), the writer and well-known epicure Joseph Wechsberg calls chef Fernand Point's La Pyramide "the best restaurant in France and perhaps anywhere." In his critique of three-star Michelin restaurants, he states that La Pyramide, "deserves at least six stars in relation to the others." Over the years, Point was host to the rich and famous. Kings, princes, movie stars, and politicians traveled to the town of Vienne where La Pyramide was located, usually not just once but time and again.

Considered the father of modern French cuisine, Point trained a generation of French master chefs, including Paul Bocuse, Alain Chapel, Louis Outhier, Raymond Thuilier, and the brothers Jean and Pierre Troisgros. Point's genius lay in his decision to veer from the dictums of his classical French training and to follow his culinary intuition instead. In doing so, he created lighter, fresher, more seasonal food that he thought was appropriate for the time. Point was also the first chef to leave the kitchen and enter the dining room; he visited with his customers and helped them compose their meals, all the while radiating the warmth and infectious humor that, along with his food, helped make La Pyramide one of the most popular restaurants in the world.

A reservation was hard to come by. The restaurant had only fifty seats; when that number was reached, the president of France himself was not allowed to enter. Point was uncompromising. Even the smallest details had to be perfect no matter what the cost: Limoges china and Baccarat crystal were the best that money could buy, as were the flowers, and, above all, the ingredients used in his kitchen. Point often said, "I'm not hard to please; I'm content with the very best."

Called "The Pharoah of the Pyramide at Vienne" by his biographer Felix Benoit, Point is remembered for his maxims along with his food. He jotted down his thoughts on cuisine and life in a small cream-colored notebook. These notes represent his gastronomic philosophy and outline the conduct he expected of young chefs. The edited notebook became known as *Ma Gastronomie*. Point's culinary wisdom included:

When one thinks of *la grande cuisine* one cannot think of money;
the two are incompatible. *La grande cuisine* is extremely expensive—but that does
not mean one cannot do very good cooking with inexpensive ingredients.

La grande cuisine *must not wait for the guest;*
it's the guest who must wait for la grande cuisine.

Before judging a thin man, one must get some information.
Perhaps he was once fat.

Garnishes must go well together, as a tie goes with a suit.

A good meal must be as harmonious as a symphony and
as well-constructed as a Norman cathedral.

What is a béarnaise sauce? An egg yolk, some shallots, some tarragon.
But believe me, it requires years of practice for the result to be perfect!
Take your eyes off it for an instant and it will be unusable.

One of the most important things that distinguishes man from other animals
is that man can get pleasure from drinking without being thirsty.

Success is the sum of a lot of small things done correctly.

Butter! Give me butter! Always butter.

The Gascon marriage of prunes and Armagnac; the Spanish ice cream made from prunes and oloroso sherry; the traditional British Christmas dessert of prunes spiked with port, lemon, and cinnamon; an Italian cake that combines chocolate, prunes, and grappa; Ali-Bab's recipe joining prunes with a licorice-flavored liqueur; Jane Grigson's recipes containing prunes and Vouvray . . . the list is endless. The pairing of spirits with fruit in general, and prunes specifically, is centuries old. The heat of the alcohol accentuates the succulence and the musky, deep, and mysterious flavor nuances of this particular fruit. Fernand Point's Pruneaux au Pichet includes both a red port and a red Bordeaux, the use of two different wines providing the dish with additional complexity.

Point created this dessert in the 1940s for the Aga Khan III, who was a frequent customer. According to Point, even when dining alone the Aga Khan consumed "a small banquet," usually enough for eight, and Point bemoaned the fact that "times have changed and such noble appetites are now rare." This provenance explains the extravagance of the two bottles of liquor. The leader of Islam once gave Point a magnificent terra-cotta vase covered with Persian motifs. From that point on, whenever the Aga Khan made the Michelin "worth a journey" trip to dine chez Point, the great chef and restaurateur reciprocated by serving him the following dessert in that very vase, which they referred to with familiarity as "le pichet." Given the Islamic prohibition against alcohol, the veracity of this story seems questionable, but, as you'll see if you make them, these drunken prunes are hard to resist.

Point served the prunes with slices of brioche mousseline (an extra-rich brioche). They really need no accompaniment, although tuiles or other crispy cookies are nice. The recipe uses about half a bottle each of both port and Bordeaux. If you do not have a use for the extra wine, you can double the recipe as the prunes will keep almost indefinitely in the refrigerator and are an impressive dessert to have on hand for unexpected guests.

Serves 8 to 10

Begin this recipe at least 48 hours before serving, because of the two 24-hour periods of soaking. The prunes are even better if the second soaking lasts a few days.

40 large prunes, pitted
16 ounces (about half a bottle) red port
16 ounces (about half a bottle) light red Bordeaux
2 cups sugar
½ vanilla bean, split and scraped
Small pinch of salt
Cold heavy cream (approximately 1½ cups)

1. At least 2 days before serving, start soaking the prunes in the port; the prunes should soak for at least 24 hours at room temperature. Soak in a glass or ceramic bowl covered with plastic wrap. The prunes develop more flavor the longer they soak.

2. Place the prunes and their soaking liquid in a nonreactive saucepan, along with the Bordeaux, sugar, vanilla bean and its seeds, and salt.

3. Bring to a simmer over high heat. Lower the heat and simmer, until the prunes are soft and a few of them are just beginning to fall apart, about 7 minutes.

4. Let the fruit cool, and then refrigerate in a covered bowl for at least 24 hours and up to 2 months (or much longer).

5. To serve, place the prunes in a glass bowl (or individual glass bowls) or in a pitcher, and cover with cold heavy cream. The prunes should be served very cold.

Apple Charlotte

The Apple Charlotte is a homey dish, and one of the many British desserts that emerged from the need to use up old bread. It consists of puréed fruit—originally apples, though pear and apricot soon became popular also—baked in a bread-lined round metal mold with slightly flared sides, this mold now also called a charlotte.

The dessert first appeared in England in the late 1700s. The origin of the name is debated. Possibly it derived from old English where a "charlyt" was a "dish of custard." Or it may be named for Queen Charlotte, the wife of England's George III and a great patron of apple growers. It is usually served warm accompanied by a cold crème anglaise. The combination of the crunchy buttered toast, the dense, liquor-laced fruit purée, and the smooth, rich vanilla crème anglaise is hard to beat.

Serves 6 to 8

6½ pounds crisp apples (a mixture of kinds—such as McIntosh, Granny Smith, Gala, Fuji, Jonagold—is the most flavorful but not necessary)
1 vanilla bean, split and scraped
1 large piece of lemon zest
4 tablespoons (½ stick) unsalted butter, plus about 12 tablespoons melted unsalted butter for the bread
Large pinch of salt

2 tablespoons dark rum, Calvados, Armagnac, or Cognac
About ¼ cup sugar, or to taste
1 rectangular loaf of fine-grained white bread or *pain de mie*, crusts removed, cut into ¼-inch slices
Jam Sauce (see page 45)
Crème Anglaise (see page 190), sweetened whipped cream, a pitcher of heavy cream, or vanilla or cinnamon ice cream

1. Peel, core, and quarter the apples. Slice them thinly and place them in a large, heavy, nonreactive saucepan or casserole with the vanilla bean and its seeds, the lemon zest, the 4 tablespoons of butter, and the salt. Cover and cook over low heat, stirring often, until the apples are soft and have broken down, 30 to 40 minutes. If the mixture dries out before the apples are soft, add 1 to 2 tablespoons water.

2. Stir in the liqueur and ¼ cup of the sugar. Continue to cook, uncovered, over medium-high heat, stirring often, until the mixture is very, very thick and can hold its shape. This will probably take at least an hour more. Near the end, stir almost constantly so the mixture does not burn. It must be thick—virtually all the water should be evaporated. If it is not thick enough at this point, the finished charlotte will collapse when it is unmolded.

3. Taste and add more sugar if necessary. The purée should remain a bit tart. Remove the vanilla bean and the lemon zest. The apples can be prepared up to this point several days ahead, cooled, covered, and refrigerated until you are ready to use them.

4. Use a cookie cutter or a glass to cut 2- to 3-inch circles out of some of the bread slices. Dip the bread circles in the melted butter and use them to line the bottom of a 6-cup charlotte mold, overlapping the slices. Cut the remaining bread slices into strips about 1½ inches wide, dip them in butter, and fit them vertically and overlapping around the inner circumference of the mold. Cut the ends off flush with the top of the mold. Save some bread to cover the top after filling the mold with the apples. The mold can be lined early in the day and set aside until you are ready to fill and bake it.

5. When ready to bake, bring the applesauce to room temperature if it has been refrigerated. Preheat the oven to 425 degrees. Fill the mold very full (it will sink as it cools) with the applesauce and place more overlapping butter-dipped bread slices on the top. Bake until the bread is golden brown, about 30 to 40 minutes. Check by placing a knife between the bread and the sides of the mold and peeking. Remove from the oven and let cool for 25 minutes on a wire rack. Invert the mold onto a serving plate. Lift the mold up a few inches to see if the dessert is firm. If not, do not risk collapse, but rather wait 10 minutes and try again. It will firm up as it cools.

6. Serve hot, warm, or at room temperature, with Jam Sauce and/or Crème Anglaise on the side.

Chocolate Torrone Loaf

Immediately after college, I moved to Cambridge, Massachusetts, and took up residence on Harvard Street in a one-bedroom apartment recently vacated by a friend who left me his furniture, rugs, dishes, and an odd assortment of pots and pans. I jammed a couple of graduation gift Le Creuset pieces into the tiny afterthought of a kitchen and prepared to teach myself to cook.

Like almost everyone else back then who was serious about home cooking, I began with Julia Child. After I had cooked my way through every single recipe in *Mastering the Art of French Cooking*, someone told me about *Michael Field's Cooking School*, a compilation of carefully chosen recipes from Field's Manhattan classes, accompanied by clear, precise, unintimidating instructions. I became an acolyte overnight.

Field was a concert pianist turned cookbook writer and cooking teacher. In the late 1950s and early 1960s he enjoyed a brief stint as a restaurateur, for several seasons running the summer restaurant at Maidstone Arms in East Hampton. Until his death in 1972, Field was the general editor of the Time-Life Foods of the World cookbook series, for which he wrote several volumes. It is commonly accepted that only his untimely death kept him from maintaining the equal footing he occupied in his lifetime alongside contemporaries such as James Beard, Craig Claiborne, and Julia Child. He was acknowledged by his students and his peers as a truly great teacher. He believed strongly in the accessibility of good cooking, and in the introduction to *Michael Field's Cooking School* he wrote:

> As a teacher, I have little patience with the concept of cooking as a mysterious art available only to the talented few. And, as a concert pianist, I have too long been confronted with the imponderables of art not to be grateful for the certainties of cooking . . . Given a love for fine food, a palate of some sensibility and sound instructions, anyone, I am convinced, can learn to cook well.

Chocolate Torrone Loaf was the first Michael Field recipe I ever made, and I continue to make it and teach it in my classes to this day. Field called this "a rich dessert in the most extravagant Italian tradition." This type of chocolate and nut dessert was popular in the nineteenth century and first half of the twentieth. The Chocolate Torrone Loaf is similar to the French *turinois*, though the latter includes chestnut purée instead of grated almonds and Kirsch instead of rum. Field's dessert benefits from these small differences, and the addition of crunchy Petits Beurre biscuits gives it an interesting and unusual texture. The Torrone Loaf is essentially an elegant and sophisticated, no-baking-necessary, version of a Nestlé Crunch bar. Cut thin slices, as a little goes a long way, especially when garnished with whipped cream. Field calls the whipped cream garnish optional. I agree it is an indulgence, but I see it as a necessary one.

Serves 10

½ pound semisweet chocolate, cut into small pieces
4 tablespoons dark rum
1 cup (2 sticks) unsalted butter, at room temperature
2 tablespoons superfine sugar
2 large eggs, separated, at room temperature
1½ cups finely ground toasted almonds
Pinch of salt
12 Social Tea or Petits Beurre biscuits, cut into
    1-by-½-inch pieces, (don't worry if they are messy,
    but discard crumbs)
Confectioners' sugar, for dusting
½ cup very cold heavy cream, whipped to soft peaks

1. In the top of a double boiler or in a metal bowl set over a saucepan of simmering water, melt the chocolate with the rum, stirring frequently. Set aside to cool to room temperature.

2. Using an electric mixer, cream the butter and the sugar. Add the egg yolks, one at a time. Blend completely, then add the almonds, followed by the completely cooled chocolate.

3. Using an electric mixer fitted with the whisk attachment, beat the egg whites together with the salt until soft peaks form. Fold the whites into the chocolate mixture until all the white has disappeared, then gently fold in the biscuit pieces.

4. Lightly grease a 1½-quart loaf pan with tasteless vegetable oil such as canola and spoon in the chocolate mixture. Rap the pan sharply to eliminate any air bubbles. Cover it tightly with plastic wrap or aluminum foil and refrigerate, preferably overnight, until quite firm (at least 4 hours).

5. To unmold, carefully run a small knife around the sides of the pan, then dip the bottom in a shallow pan of hot water for 15 seconds. Quickly invert it onto a chilled rectangular or oval platter. If it does not unmold, repeat the dipping process.

6. Smooth with a knife or spatula. Return to the refrigerator for at least 10 minutes or up to 48 hours, or until ready to serve. Dust just before serving with confectioners' sugar, cut into very thin slices, and serve with dollops of chilled whipped cream.

Note: This recipe uses raw egg whites. If you are concerned about bacteria, or if serving to the young, elderly, or those with health issues, use pasteurized egg whites or liquid egg whites as a substitute. Also, there's less risk of bacteria with organic eggs.

CAKES

James Beard's Venetian Fruitcake

La Fonda's Pudding Cake

The Brown Derby's Orange Chiffon Cake

Fernand Point's Marjolaine, "Le Succès"

Blum's Coffee Crunch Cake

Chasen's Banana Shortcake with Banana Sauce

The Four Seasons's Christmas Fruitcake

Miss Grimble's Chocolate and Orange Marbled Cheesecake

Cassata Siciliana

La Galette des Rois

The Trident's Carrot Cake

Zausner's Crème Fraîche Cheesecake

Windows on the World's Chocolate Pastry Cake

Scandia's Princess Cake

George Lang's Dobos Torte

The Vicomte de Mauduit's Neapolitan Cake

JAMES BEARD'S

Venetian Fruitcake

J ames Beard, the acknowledged dean of American cooking, was born in 1903. By the time he
died, in 1985, he was hailed as "The Father of American Gastronomy." Beard wrote more than
twenty books on food and cooking and hundreds of articles. He traveled the country as a food
authority disseminating his message of top-quality ingredients, honestly prepared. This recipe
comes by way of brilliant food writer and teacher Barbara Kafka, who taught with Beard and in
The James Beard Celebration Cookbook (1990) wrote: "James Beard was one of the giants of American food. . . . He had a Rabelasian laugh and a fierce temper. He had the gift of enthusiasm in speech
and writing. . . . He wanted everybody to cook . . . to make cooking their work, and to involve each
new friend in his large world of past and present friends." Kafka got this recipe directly from Beard
and is fairly sure it came from one of his classes. Beard prefaced his printed recipe with the following:

"While I was in Venice, I discovered fruitcake in a bakeshop made with polenta, or cornmeal,
bought some and fell madly in love with it. Try as I would, I couldn't find anyone who had the recipe.
The bakery gave me some very vague directions. When I got home, I experimented. After four or
five tries, I had it down pat. Someone in Venice told me this was often the celebration cake eaten
on Twelfth Night, like the *galette des rois* in France, and it makes a perfect holiday cake here
because it's fruity and luscious but not too rich."

The subtle crunch of the cornmeal makes this cake unusual and just as appealing for breakfast
(toasted or not) as it is for tea or after dinner with a glass of Vin Santo.

Serves 8

1½ cups all-purpose flour, plus additional for the fruit

1 tablespoon baking powder

1 cup yellow cornmeal

½ teaspoon salt

½ cup chopped candied fruit

½ cup mixed raisins and currants, and/or chopped dried
figs, apricots, peaches

1 cup (2 sticks) unsalted butter, at room temperature

1 cup sugar

3 large eggs, at room temperature

2 tablespoons Cognac

1. Preheat the oven to 350 degrees. Butter a 9-inch
springform pan. Line the bottom with parchment paper;
butter the paper.

2. Sift together the 1½ cups flour, baking powder, cornmeal, and salt. Set aside.

3. Toss the candied fruit and raisins and currants with
flour to coat. Shake off the excess. Set aside.

4. Using an electric mixer, cream the butter and sugar
until very light and fluffy, about 5 minutes. Add the eggs,
one at a time, beating well after each addition. Beat in
the flour mixture, blending well. Fold in the candied fruits

and raisins and currants, along with the Cognac. Make sure the fruit is evenly distributed. Spoon the batter into the prepared pan. Lift the pan a few inches off the counter and drop it on the counter once or twice to settle the batter and remove any air bubbles.

5. Bake until the cake is just beginning to pull away from the sides of the pan and a cake tester inserted into the center comes out clean, about 45 to 50 minutes. Do not overbake. Let cool in the pan for 10 minutes, then invert the cake onto your hand or a plate and quickly reinvert it onto a wire rack. The cake will keep for a week if wrapped in plastic and refrigerated. Freeze for longer storage. Let it reach room temperature before serving.

LA FONDA'S

Pudding Cake

Will Rogers was reported to have said that Fred Harvey "kept the West in food and wives." The visionary immigrant from England was often called the "Civilizer of the West." As the United States expanded toward the Pacific, he filled a vacuum in recognizing the need for quality restaurants to serve the passengers on those westbound trains. Before Harvey, the only options were roadhouses where the food was greasy, overpriced, and served so slowly that diners often had no time to finish their meals before returning to their trains. These poor conditions often discouraged railroad travel. Fred Harvey changed all that.

This forward-thinking entrepreneur opened his first restaurant in 1876 in Topeka, Kansas. Two years later he began a partnership with the Atchison, Topeka, and Santa Fe Railway and, in 1889, the railway gave Harvey exclusive rights to manage and operate restaurants, hotels, and, later, dining car service on all its railroads west of the Missouri. His business soon expanded to serve most of the rail lines in the west.

By the turn of the century, Harvey's establishments and dining car service, with their excellent, reasonably priced food, cleanliness, and friendly, flawless service, were the epitome of American elegance. At its peak in the 1930s, the Harvey Company was serving fifteen million meals a year. Harvey's most revolutionary dining car innovation was a system that allowed a full train of passengers to eat an impeccably served four-course meal in thirty minutes. This accomplishment was primarily attributable to the famous Harvey Girls (rendered even more famous by the 1946 film of the same name starring Angela Lansbury, Ray Bolger, Cyd Charisse, and Judy Garland, and featuring the Oscar-winning song "On the Atchison, Topeka, and the Santa Fe"). Their history began when Harvey decided to hire only female waitstaff after becoming dissatisfied with the conduct of his unruly male servers. As the West did not easily attract the type of young lady Fred Harvey wanted to hire, he put ads in newspapers throughout the East and Midwest seeking single, well-mannered, neat, and educated, "Young women, 18 to 30 years of age, of good character, attractive and intelligent." The response was huge. These undauntable girls doubtless had a sense of adventure, but they had to abide by strict rules. Living in chaperoned dormitories above the station houses, they worked long hours, often getting up in the middle of the night to meet trains. Each girl wore a uniform—a black dress and a starched white apron, stockings, and shoes—which had to be immaculate at all times. Trained to the exacting standards Harvey expected of them, the Harvey Girls were exemplary models of efficiency and comportment.

This light and homey "pudding" cake is studded with walnuts, delightful in its simplicity and unusual in its use of graham cracker crumbs instead of flour. It was served by the now-legendary Harvey Girls on Fred Harvey's railroad dining cars, in the Harvey Houses, as well as at the Harvey La Fonda Hotel on the Plaza in Santa Fe, New Mexico. As a child, I remember looking forward to and then ordering it repeatedly while on the train en route from Los Angeles to Santa Fe.

La Fonda Pudding Cake is a great family-style dessert. Serve it after an all-American dinner of meatloaf, roast chicken, grilled steak, or roast pork. Cut it in squares, dust with powdered sugar, and accompany with a dollop of whipped cream or vanilla ice cream. (It's also good for breakfast with fresh fruit and plain or vanilla yogurt.)

Serves 8

4 large eggs, separated, at room temperature
1 cup sugar
1 teaspoon vanilla extract
12 double graham crackers (24 single squares), pulverized or very finely crushed
½ cup finely chopped toasted walnuts
1 teaspoon baking powder
¼ teaspoon cream of tartar
⅛ teaspoon salt
Whipped cream and additional chopped toasted walnuts to serve (optional)

1. Preheat the oven to 350 degrees. Butter and flour an 8-inch square cake pan and line the bottom with parchment paper; butter the paper.
2. Using an electric mixer, beat the egg yolks, ¾ cup of the sugar, and the vanilla until light and fluffy, about 10 minutes, scraping the sides of the bowl frequently with a rubber spatula.
3. Mix the graham cracker crumbs, walnuts, and baking powder together in a small bowl, then turn the contents of the bowl into the egg yolk mixture and stir to combine.
4. Using an electric mixer fitted with the whisk attachment, beat the egg whites with the cream of tartar and the salt until soft peaks form. Gradually add the remaining ¼ cup sugar, continuing to beat.
5. Fold ¼ of the egg white mixture into the egg yolk mixture until well blended, then fold in the remaining whites. The batter will be very stiff.
6. Pour the batter into the prepared pan and bake until the cake is just beginning to pull away from the sides of the pan and a cake tester inserted into the center comes out clean, about 30 to 35 minutes.
7. Let the cake cool for 10 minutes in the pan, then invert onto a serving plate. The cake can be served at room temperature, but it is best served warm with whipped cream and chopped toasted walnuts.

Orange Chiffon Cake

No other restaurants are as closely associated with Hollywood's Golden Age as those in the Brown Derby chain. Famous for inventing the Cobb Salad, the original hat-shaped restaurant on Wilshire Boulevard was for a time the symbol of Los Angeles itself.

How the Brown Derby got its name is a subject of some speculation. According to *The Brown Derby Cookbook*, the creation of the first restaurant was the result of an offhand remark. One evening in 1925, Herbert K. Somborn, a major Hollywood producer and ex-husband of Gloria Swanson, was chatting with Abe Frank, at the time the manager of Los Angeles's Ambassador Hotel, and Sid Grauman of Chinese Theater fame. Commenting on the dearth of acceptable restaurants in the L.A. area, one of them said, "You could open a restaurant in an alley and call it anything, and if the food and service were good, the patrons would come flocking." There is another version of the story in which someone supposedly said, "You could call it something as silly as a brown derby if the food were good enough," and yet another in which a friend of Somborn's said, "If you know anything about food, you can sell it out of a hat." Somborn took one or more of these comments to heart, along with taking Jack Warner as a silent partner. The following year the first Brown Derby opened its doors. Celebrities including Mary Pickford, Humphrey Bogart, Loretta Young, and Wallace Beery (another ex-husband of Gloria Swanson) poured in and remained loyal patrons for years to come. Other devoted customers were visitors from New York, who were happy to find a restaurant that stayed open twenty-four hours.

The first dessert on the menu when the original Brown Derby opened was the now-famous chiffon cake, invented in 1927 by Henry Baker, a sixty-four-year-old insurance salesman who baked on the side for Hollywood parties. It was hailed as the first truly new cake since angel food, invented a century earlier. Baker had created an exceptionally moist and tender cake, "light as chiffon" and "rich as a butter." He attributed the special properties of his cake — among other things, it could be cut into individual portions while still frozen and thawed quickly — to a "mysterious" ingredient, which remained a secret for twenty years. In 1947, when Baker sold his recipe to Betty Crocker and General Mills, the secret ingredient was revealed to be nothing more exotic than vegetable oil. The flour company heavily promoted the "glamorous cake made with salad oil," and very soon both Baker and his cake were famous nationwide. And rightfully so. Chiffon cakes in their many different flavors are light, flavorful, and versatile. They can be iced or not; they pair well in summer with fresh seasonal fruits, and in cooler months with poached apples, pears, or quince and cooked fruit compotes. They are delicious with custards, ice creams, whipped cream, crème anglaise, and most dessert sauces.

Serves 8 to 10

For the orange chiffon cake:
2¼ cups sifted cake flour
1¼ cups superfine sugar
1 tablespoon baking powder
1 teaspoon salt
5 large eggs, separated, plus 3 whites, at room
    temperature
½ cup tasteless vegetable oil such as canola
3 tablespoons grated orange zest
1½ teaspoons vanilla extract
½ teaspoon cream of tartar
¼ cup granulated sugar

For the orange icing:
6 tablespoons unsalted butter
3 cups confectioners' sugar, sifted
3 tablespoons freshly squeezed orange juice
Grated zest of 2 large oranges
⅛ teaspoon salt
½ teaspoon vanilla extract

To make the orange chiffon cake:
1. Preheat the oven to 325 degrees.
2. Into a large bowl, sift together the flour, superfine sugar, baking powder, and salt. Sift again.
3. Using an electric mixer fitted with the whisk attachment, beat the 5 egg yolks, oil, orange zest, vanilla, and ¾ cup water on high speed until smooth. Gradually add the flour mixture and beat on low until just combined.
4. Using the electric mixer fitted with the whisk attachment, beat the 8 egg whites on medium speed until foamy. Add the cream of tartar and beat until very soft peaks form. Gradually add the granulated sugar and increase the speed to high. Beat until peaks are stiff but not dry.

5. Using a rubber spatula, fold one quarter of the egg whites into the egg yolk–flour mixture. Pour the egg mixture over the remaining egg whites and fold together until just combined. Scrape the batter into an ungreased 10-inch tube or angel food cake pan with a removable bottom. Smooth the top and bake in the lower third of the oven until the top springs back when lightly pressed and a cake tester inserted in the center comes out clean, 55 to 65 minutes; check after 30 minutes. If the cake is browning too quickly, lightly rest a piece of foil over it.
6. Cool upside down on a bottle, with the bottle neck through the hole, until completely cool, at least 1½ hours.
7. To unmold, slide a thin knife around the cake to detach it from the pan, pressing the knife against the pan to avoid tearing the cake. Use the knife to detach the cake from the center tube: pull the tube upward to remove the cake from the pan side. Slide the knife under the cake to detach it from the bottom. Invert and let the cake drop onto your hand or a serving platter. Invert again, right side up, on a rack to cool completely.

To make the orange icing:
1. In a medium saucepan, melt the butter over low heat. Remove from the heat and stir in the confectioners' sugar, orange juice and zest, and salt.
2. Turn the heat down as low as possible and return the saucepan to the heat. Cook for 5 minutes, stirring constantly. Remove from the heat and beat (briefly for a pourable glaze or several minutes for spreadable icing). You can place the saucepan in a larger pan of ice water to speed the process.
3. Stir in the vanilla and drizzle the glaze over or spread the icing on the cake. Let set before serving.

Marjolaine "Le Succès"

It took Point twenty-six years and hundreds of pounds of ingredients to perfect this marjolaine, which he considered to be one of his masterpieces. A "marjolaine" is a long, rectangular dacquoise (a cake made with alternating layers of nut meringue and whipped cream or buttercream) using a mixture of hazelnuts and almonds to flavor the meringue and chocolate buttercream as a filling. A "succès" is the same almond and hazelnut meringue, but layered with praline buttercream. A brilliant creation, Point's "Le Succès" consists of three different flavors of buttercream layered between four rectangles of almond-hazelnut meringue and iced with chocolate. It was a favorite and rarely off the menu at La Pyramide, where Point's cake was four times the size of this one, large enough to serve both the lunch and dinner guests.

For facility and variety, though a deviation from Point's original concept, you can triple the amount of one of the buttercreams instead of making all three flavors, or replace the buttercream with ice cream (one flavor or three). If you use ice cream, put the cake together, then freeze it for at least an hour. Remove the cake from the freezer and quickly frost it with the chocolate buttercream (in this case you need to make only half the recipe), and refreeze for at least twenty minutes before serving. If rock-hard, let the cake soften a bit before slicing; fifteen minutes or so at room temperature should do it. Garnish with fresh or candy violets if you want a bit of extra elegance. Plan ahead, as this cake must be refrigerated twenty-four hours before serving.

Serves 10 to 12

For the meringue-nut layers:
8 large egg whites, at room temperature
¼ teaspoon cream of tartar
Large pinch of salt
1½ cups blanched almonds, toasted
1 cup hazelnuts, toasted and skinned
1⅓ cups superfine sugar
¼ cup all-purpose flour, sifted

For the chocolate buttercream icing:
12 ounces semisweet chocolate, chopped
8 ounces crème fraîche or sour cream

For the vanilla and praline buttercreams:
2 cups cold heavy cream
¼ cup superfine sugar
1½ teaspoons vanilla extract
4 tablespoons (½ stick) unsalted butter,
    at room temperature
4 ounces Praline Powder (recipe follows)

For the garnish:
Shaved semisweet chocolate (optional)
Confectioners' sugar, for dusting (optional)
Fresh or candy violets or other edible flowers (optional)

To make the meringue-nut layers:
1. Preheat the oven to 325 degrees. Draw a 12-by-16-inch rectangle on a piece of parchment paper and turn the paper over onto a baking sheet. Butter and flour the paper.
2. Using an electric mixer fitted with the whisk attachment, beat the egg whites together with the cream of tartar and salt until stiff.
3. Combine the nuts, superfine sugar, and flour.
4. Lightly fold the nut mixture into the egg whites.
5. Spread the mixture evenly into a rectangle, slightly larger than the one drawn on the parchment paper (so it can be trimmed and cut into 4-by-12-inch rectangles after baking).
6. Bake for 45 minutes, or until the meringue is crisp on top but still pliable.
7. Slide the paper with the meringue off the baking sheet. Let cool on a wire rack. Trim the meringue to exactly 12 by 16 inches and then remove the paper. Using a ruler, measure and then carefully, with a serrated knife, cut the meringue into four perfectly even 4-by-12-inch rectangles. Set aside. Once cool, the meringue can be wrapped in foil and stored at room temperature for at least 3 days.

To make the chocolate buttercream icing:
1. Melt the chocolate in a saucepan set over the lowest possible heat, stirring constantly. When melted, stir in the crème fraîche or sour cream; then, continuing to stir, bring to a boil. Remove from the heat as soon as it boils. Beat until cool and of spreading consistency (this is easier to do using an electric mixer). Set aside while you make the two other buttercreams.

To make the vanilla and praline buttercreams:
1. Whip the cream together with the superfine sugar and vanilla until soft peaks form; set aside.
2. Using an electric mixer, cream the butter well, at least 5 minutes, then add the whipped cream a little at a time until the butter will not absorb any more cream.
3. Divide the mixture in half and beat the praline powder into one of the portions. Assemble the cake or refrigerate the buttercreams for up to 3 days, bringing to spreading consistency before continuing.

To assemble the cake:
1. Lay one of the meringue-nut rectangles on a platter and spread it with a thick layer of chocolate icing, reserving the rest to ice the finished cake. If the icing is too thin to spread, refrigerate it for a few minutes, then beat again. If it is too thick, place the bowl over very low heat or dip it in hot water for a few seconds, then beat.
2. Top the chocolate icing with a second meringue-nut layer and spread it with all of the vanilla buttercream.
3. Top with the third meringue-nut layer and spread with all of the praline buttercream.
4. Top with the fourth meringue-nut layer and refrigerate for at least 30 minutes.
5. Ice the entire cake with the remaining chocolate icing (which may need rebeating, heating, cooling, and so on), or ice just the top and let the layers show on the sides. Press some shaved chocolate onto the iced sides and/or top, if desired, and top with the candy or edible fresh flowers, if using.
6. Refrigerate the cake for 24 hours. Just before serving, dust the top with confectioners' sugar.

PRALINE POWDER

1 cup sugar
⅛ teaspoon cream of tartar
1 cup blanched almonds or skinned hazelnuts or a mixture, lightly toasted

1. Lightly oil a baking sheet with tasteless vegetable oil or butter.
2. Put the sugar, cream of tartar, and ½ cup water in a saucepan and stir over low heat until the sugar dissolves. Insert a candy thermometer. Cook, without stirring, until the mixture is a medium-dark caramel, deep gold or light brown in color, 360 to 370 degrees on a candy thermometer.
3. Stir in the nuts and immediately remove the pan from the heat. Immediately pour the nut mixture onto the prepared baking sheet and let cool completely.
4. Break into small pieces and pulverize in a food processor or crush with a rolling pin. The Praline Powder can be stored in an airtight container at room temperature for a month or in the freezer for at least a year.

Coffee Crunch Cake

A forest of lemonade trees bearing lollipop fruit is my most vivid memory of the the Blum's of my earliest childhood (located in Beverly Hills, this was the first Blum's outside San Francisco). Small round glass tables with delicate floral wrought-iron bases and matching chairs, garden furniture–like, were placed under and around the trees. It was a bit like dining in Hobbit-land, a child's fantasy made real. A few years passed, and the restaurant moved to Wilshire Boulevard. The lemonade trees were history, as were the charming little tables and chairs—all of it replaced by a more sanitized and conventional décor: booths featuring dark pink leatherette banquettes and pale pink formica tables. Despite the departure of the magical setting, the soda shop menu remained perfect and the same—salads and sandwiches, followed by those famous desserts and candies, including luscious cakes, elaborate ice cream sundae and parfait creations, coffee toffee pie, almondettes, and much more.

My mother did not allow herself or encourage her children to sink into sugar gluttony. Thus my favorite dessert adventures as a child were embarked on when my Aunt Iva or my grandmother visited from out of town. Sometimes Iva drove me to the nation's very first Baskin-Robbins 31 Flavors, which had opened virtually around the corner from Blum's. We would hop out, purchase small containers of each of that day's thirty-one flavors, and then sit in the parked car eating and critiquing until every last bite was gone.

Despite my love of all that ice cream, Blum's Coffee Crunch Cake was my favorite childhood treat. It's still way up there on my list of the "Top Ten." The recipe here is adapted from one published in the *San Francisco Chronicle* in the 1970s and sent to me years ago by Aunt Iva. I add coffee to the vanilla whipped cream to intensify the cake's coffee flavor and I apply two layers of the coffee crunch rather than one: a layer of crunch applied several hours before serving absorbs moisture from the whipped cream and becomes unexpectedly and wonderfully chewy, while a second layer pressed into the icing just before serving provides the anticipated "crunch."

I typically ordered the cake à la mode with coffee ice cream. When my grandmother was feeling particularly indulgent, she let me order a piece of the cake *and* a Coffiesta Sundae, my second favorite Blum's dessert. To sample this delicious ice cream concoction at home, make extra crunch (wrapped airtight and stored in a dry place, it should keep for several months) and serve an abundant amount of it over coffee ice cream first topped with hot fudge sauce (see the C. C. Brown's Hot Fudge Sauce recipe, page 150) and a huge dollop of whipped cream. Absolute perfection.

Serves 10 to 12

For the crunch:
1½ cups sugar
¼ cup strong brewed coffee
¼ cup light corn syrup
1 tablespoon baking soda, sifted

For the cake:
6 large eggs, separated, at room temperature
1 teaspoon finely grated lemon zest
1 cup sugar
¼ cup hot strong brewed coffee
1 tablespoon fresh lemon juice
1 teaspoon vanilla extract
1 cup sifted cake flour
1½ teaspoons baking powder
¼ teaspoon salt
1 teaspoon cream of tartar

For the coffee whipped cream:
3 cups very cold heavy cream
1 tablespoon vanilla extract
3 tablespoons sugar (superfine is preferable)
1½ teaspoons coffee extract or 1 tablespoon instant
    espresso powder, such as Medaglia D'Oro

To make the crunch:
1. In a saucepan at least 5 inches deep, combine the sugar, coffee, and corn syrup.
2. Cook over medium heat, stirring just until the sugar dissolves. Stop stirring and insert a candy thermometer. Cook until the thermometer registers 290 degrees. Toward the end of cooking, around 270 to 280 degrees, stir occasionally to prevent the mixture from scorching.
3. Immediately remove from the heat and stir in the baking soda. Be prepared; the mixture will bubble up. Stir thoroughly and vigorously.
4. Pour into a 9-inch (or a bit larger) square pan. Do not move the crunch at all until cool or it may deflate.
5. When ready to use, remove the crunch from the pan and crush with a rolling pin to form large and small pieces, the biggest of which should be about ½ inch. Set aside.

To make the cake:
1. Preheat the oven to 350 degrees.
2. Using an electric mixer, beat the egg yolks together with the lemon zest and sugar until light and fluffy, about 5 minutes. Beat in the hot coffee and then the lemon juice and vanilla.
3. Sift the flour together with the baking powder and salt and gradually add to the egg yolk mixture. Beat just until well combined.
4. Using an electric mixer fitted with the whisk attachment, beat the egg whites on low speed until foamy, slowly increasing the mixer speed; add the cream of tartar and beat until stiff but not dry.
5. Pour the egg yolk–flour mixture over the egg whites and fold together until just blended. Pour the batter into an ungreased angel food cake pan. Smooth the top with a spatula and bake in the lower third of the oven for 45 to 55 minutes, or until the cake springs back when lightly pressed and a cake tester comes out clean. Cool the cake with the pan turned upside down over a bottle.
6. To unmold, slide a thin knife around the edges of the cake to detach it from the pan, pressing the knife against the pan to avoid tearing the cake; detach the cake from the center tube by pulling the tube upward to remove the cake from the pan side. Slide the knife under the cake to detach it from the bottom. Invert and allow the cake to drop onto a rack or a serving platter. Invert again, right side up, on a rack to cool completely.
7. Split the cake horizontally into three equal layers.

To make the coffee whipped cream:
1. In a chilled bowl, whisk together the cream, vanilla, sugar, and coffee flavoring until soft peaks form.

To assemble the cake:
1. Place a cake layer on a serving platter. Generously spread some of the coffee whipped cream on it and add some of the smaller pieces of the crunch. Place the middle layer on top, and add the whipped cream and crunch. Place the top layer over this. Ice the cake using the rest of the whipped cream and put smaller pieces of crunch on the top and sides of the cake. Reserve the rest of the crunch for later. Refrigerate until 1 hour before serving (if the weather is very hot leave it in the fridge).
2. When ready to serve, pat all of the remaining crunch onto the sides and top.
3. Serve plain or, even better, with coffee or vanilla ice cream.

Banana Shortcake

WITH BANANA SAUCE

"What do you think the odds would be that a baby born of poor parents in Odessa in southwest Russia in 1898 would one day wind up in Beverly Hills, California, rich, famous, and loved by some of the most celebrated people on earth?" So said Jimmy Stewart in 1973 of Dave Chasen, the founder of Chasen's, Stewart's favorite restaurant. When Chasen's closed its doors in 1995, it had been open fifty-nine years and outlived all the city's other legendary eateries—the Brown Derby, La Rue, Perino's, Scandia, Romanoff's, and Tail o' the Cock.

The story began in 1936, when ex-vaudevillian Dave Chasen borrowed $3,500 from Harold Ross, then-editor of the *New Yorker*, and opened a little barbecue shack called Chasen's Southern Pit on the corner of Doheny and Beverly Boulevard in West Hollywood, just over the Beverly Hills line. Its immediate claim to fame was serving the best chili in town. By 1940, the name had been shortened to Chasen's, and the eatery had become a gathering spot for Hollywood luminaries. It was one of the first restaurants to have "power tables" and "Siberia." In addition to Stewart, devoted regulars included Gregory Peck, Frank Sinatra, Elizabeth Taylor, Bob Hope, Clark Gable, Carole Lombard, Alfred Hitchcock, and W. C. Fields.

Chasen's was the backdrop for numerous important moments of Hollywood history. Alfred Hitchcock outlined the plot of *Notorious* over dinner with RKO producer William Dozier; Ronald Reagan proposed to Nancy; Greta Garbo made her first L.A. restaurant appearance; William Wyler convinced David Niven to play Edgar in *Wuthering Heights*; and when a certain child star begged for a drink of her own as she sat with her cocktail-drinking parents, Dave Chasen invented the Shirley Temple—ginger ale with grenadine and a slice of lemon plus a cherry.

Chasen took good care of his regulars. To accommodate Lana Turner's pregnancy, he had part of the table sawed off so she could fit into the booth. Hollywood royalty felt they could relax and be themselves at Chasen's—press, paparazzi, and autograph seekers were turned away at the door. The restaurant had a conservative décor, which contrasted sharply with its three-ring-circus atmosphere. Ray Bolger danced among the tables, James Cagney sang Yiddish songs, and Frank Morgan, the Wizard of Oz himself, occasionally climbed up on the bar to perform a striptease. Orson Welles often got beyond rowdy. During a notorious 1939 tantrum, he hurled a flaming serving dish at John Houseman, missing his target but nearly setting the restaurant on fire.

Growing up in Beverly Hills, I walked by Chasen's almost daily and well remember its forest green-trimmed white exterior and elegant green-and-white-striped awnings. In my later teens, I ate there often with my boyfriend Michael, whose father was a Hollywood mover and shaker with his own special table far from Siberia. We frequently joined his parents and their friends for Caesar salad, hobo steak, the famous chili, and Banana Shortcake with Banana Sauce. Michael's father always said this unusual shortcake was his favorite dessert.

I've adapted this recipe from Betty Goodwin's book *Chasen's, Where Hollywood Dined: Recipes and Memories*. It consists of rum-soaked pound cake layered with whipped cream and bananas, then sauced with a variation of the same—decadent and delicious, especially if you love bananas. Chasen's gilded this lily with hot fudge sauce, but I prefer it unembellished.

Chasen's served the same banana sauce over rich chocolate ice cream, a sublime combination. In this case, the drizzle of hot fudge is a good thing.

Serves 8

For the pound cake:
¼ cup milk
4 large eggs, at room temperature, lightly beaten
2 teaspoons vanilla extract
2 cups cake flour, sifted
1 cup sugar
1 teaspoon baking powder
⅜ teaspoon salt
1 cup (2 sticks) unsalted butter, softened

To assemble:
2 tablespoons rum
2 cups very cold heavy cream
¼ cup sugar (superfine is preferable)
1 teaspoon vanilla extract
5 small ripe bananas
Chasen's Banana Sauce (recipe follows)
C.C. Brown's Hot Fudge Sauce (see page 150)
    or store-bought (optional)

To make the pound cake:
1. Preheat the oven to 350 degrees. Butter a 9-by-5-inch loaf pan. Line the bottom with parchment paper; butter the paper and dust with flour.
2. Combine the milk, eggs, and vanilla in a small bowl.
3. Sift the flour, sugar, baking powder, and salt together into the bowl of an electric mixer. Add the butter and half of the egg mixture. Mix on low speed until just combined, then increase the speed to medium and beat for 1 minute.
4. Scrape down the sides of the bowl and add half of the remaining egg mixture. Beat for 30 seconds. Scrape the bowl again, add the remaining egg mixture and beat for another 30 seconds.
5. Transfer the batter to the prepared pan, smooth the top, and bake in the middle of the preheated oven for about 1 hour, until a cake tester inserted in the center comes out clean. After 40 minutes, check to see if the cake is browning too quickly; if so, cover loosely with foil.
6. Remove from the oven and place the pan on a wire rack to cool for 15 minutes. Loosen the sides of the cake with a knife or metal spatula, then invert the cake onto your hand and then back right side up onto the rack to finish cooling.

To assemble the dessert:
1. Split the cake horizontally into two equal layers. Place one layer on a serving plate. Prick with a fork and drizzle it with the 2 tablespoons of rum.
2. Using an electric mixer fitted with the whisk attachment, whip the heavy cream with the sugar and the vanilla on medium speed until soft peaks form. Spread about ⅛ of the whipped cream generously over the rum-soaked cake layer.
3. Peel 4 of the bananas and lay them in a single layer

over the whipped cream. Cover the bananas with another ⅛ of the whipped cream and top with the second layer of cake.

4. Ice the cake with the remaining whipped cream. Chill until ready to serve.

5. When ready to serve, slice the remaining banana into thin rounds and place them decoratively on the top of the cake. Slice the cake into 8 equal pieces and serve, topped with Chasen's Banana Sauce and optional hot fudge sauce. Or pass the sauces at the table.

CHASEN'S BANANA SAUCE

1 pint best-quality store-bought vanilla ice cream
    or homemade (see recipe, page 190), softened
½ cup very cold heavy cream, whipped with
    1 tablespoon sugar and ½ teaspoon vanilla extract
2 very ripe bananas, cut into very thin rounds
1 tablespoon rum, or to taste

1. Fold the softened ice cream into the whipped cream.
2. Toss the bananas with the rum and fold the fruit into the cream mixture. Serve immediately.

THE FOUR SEASONS'S

Christmas Fruitcake

During the reign of co-owners Tom Margittai and Paul Kovi, the Four Seasons restaurant in New York presented its best customers with Christmas gifts from the pastry kitchen. According to the food writer and teacher Barbara Kafka, the A+ list received Chef Kumin's exquisite handmade chocolate boxes filled with an assortment of chocolate creams, truffles, and caramels, while the A list received this sophisticated and delicious fruitcake.

In their 1980 book *The Four Seasons: The Ultimate Book of Food, Wine and Elegant Dining*, Margittai and Kovi describe the fruitcake, "We think it is very special—light in color and kept moist by a marzipan wrapping rather than by soaking it, as is usual, in brandy."

It's too bad the restaurant no longer makes this cake, but it's a tradition worth reviving. Over the holidays, try making it for your own A and A+ lists.

Makes 5 (8½-by-4-inch) loaves

11½ cups sifted bread flour
3 pounds mixed candied fruit (a combination of all or
    some of the following: orange, lemon, angelica, citron,
    pineapple and peach)
½ teaspoon salt
½ teaspoon ground cinnamon

½ teaspoon ground ginger
1 pound 10 ounces (6¼ sticks) unsalted butter,
    at room temperature
3½ cups granulated sugar, plus more for the topping
20 large eggs, at room temperature
1 vanilla bean

½ cup rum
Finely grated zest of 2 lemons
Juice of 1 lemon
2 cups coarsely chopped toasted walnuts
Confectioners' sugar
3 pounds marzipan
½ cup simple syrup (see Note)

1. Preheat the oven to 400 degrees.
2. Heavily butter and flour five 8½-by-4-inch loaf pans.
3. Toss 1 cup of the flour with the candied fruit and set aside.
4. Sift together the remaining flour, the salt, cinnamon, and ginger. Set aside.
5. Using an electric mixer, cream the butter together with the granulated sugar until light and fluffy, about 5 minutes. Add 10 of the eggs, three or four at a time, beating well after each addition. Beat in 1 cup of the flour mixture, then add the remaining eggs, again three or four at a time.
6. Add the remaining flour mixture. Split the vanilla bean lengthwise and scrape the seeds into the batter. Stir in the rum, lemon zest, and lemon juice, and blend well.
7. Fold in the candied fruit and walnuts.
8. Divide the batter evenly among the prepared pans. Tap the pans on the work surface to eliminate air bubbles. Smooth the tops with a spatula.

9. Place the pans on a baking sheet and bake in the middle of the oven until a cake tester inserted in the center comes out clean, 1 hour to 1 hour and 15 minutes. Let cool for 5 minutes, then run a knife around the sides, invert, and let the cakes cool completely on a wire rack.
10. If the tops have rounded, trim them flat with a serrated knife.
11. Sprinkle confectioners' sugar on the work surface to prevent sticking. Divide the marzipan into 5 equal pieces. Roll and trim each piece into an 8-by-14-inch rectangle.
12. Brush the rectangles with simple syrup. Place a cooled fruitcake over each marzipan piece and roll up to completely cover the cakes except for the ends.
13. Brush the tops and sides of the cakes with simple syrup and roll in granulated sugar to coat. With a knife, make a cross-hatch design on the tops and then wrap in aluminum foil to store.

Variation: An easier alternative to the rolled marzipan is marzipan icing. Triple the recipe for marzipan icing for the Scandia Princess Cake (page 121). Ice the cakes, roll in sugar, and let the cakes sit out until the icing hardens, at least several hours.

Note: To make a simple syrup, dissolve ¼ cup sugar in ½ cup water. Bring to a boil, stirring, and cook 5 minutes. Let cool.

Chocolate and Orange Marbled Cheesecake

McCall's magazine called Sylvia Balser Hirsch "the My Fair Lady of the Cheesecake World." Hirsch, aka Miss Grimble, opened her bakery in 1960s New York. By the early 1970s she had become an institution. My boyfriend and I would often make a late Sunday breakfast out of an entire Miss Grimble's cheesecake, almost always the very rich orange and chocolate concoction described below. The combination of the dense chocolate crust with the lighter chocolate cheesecake is great, and the addition of orange sends it over the top. This recipe is adapted from Hirsch's 1983 cookbook *Miss Grimble Presents Delicious Desserts*. The cheesecake marbling technique is a creation of Miss Grimble's.

"Miss Grimble" recommends garnishing the cheesecake with whipped cream perfumed with Grand Marnier or Curaçao. I prefer it on its own, or double the crust recipe and press the extra crumbs onto the top of the cake after baking and cooling. For both taste and visual appeal, drizzling two ounces of melted semisweet chocolate over the crumbs is a nice touch.

Serves 12

For the crust:
1½ cups chocolate wafer crumbs (made by pulverizing the chocolate wafers in a food processor or crushing them with a rolling pin)
4 tablespoons (½ stick) unsalted butter, melted
2 tablespoons sugar
Finely grated zest of 1 orange
1 ounce unsweetened chocolate, melted

For the filling:
40 ounces (five 8-ounce packages) cream cheese, at room temperature
1⅔ cups sugar
2½ tablespoons all-purpose flour
5 large eggs, plus 3 yolks, at room temperature
Grated zest of 2 oranges
¼ cup heavy cream
1 teaspoon vanilla extract
4 ounces unsweetened chocolate, melted

To make the crust:
1. Butter a 10-inch springform pan.
2. Blend all the crust ingredients together. (This is easiest to do using a food processor.) Press the crumb crust evenly into the bottom of the prepared pan.

To make the filling:
1. Preheat the oven to 500 degrees.
2. Using an electric mixer, combine all the filling ingredients except the melted chocolate, in the order listed, beating well after each addition. When well blended, divide the mixture in half and stir the melted chocolate into one of the halves.
3. Place the plain and chocolate batters in 2 separate 2-cup measures. Hold the two handles together in one hand and pour the two batters together, in a swirling fashion, over the crust in the pan, to create a marbleized effect.
4. Place the pan on a baking sheet and bake in the middle of the oven for 10 minutes. Lower the oven temperature to 200 degrees and bake another 1 to 1½ hours, until the center of the cheesecake is just set. Turn off the oven and leave the cheesecake inside to cool, about 3 hours. Refrigerate. Remove from the refrigerator about 20 minutes before you are ready to serve it, then remove the sides of the pan. The cheesecake should be served cool but not right out of the refrigerator.

Cassata Siciliana

Sicily has been a cradle of gastronomy for two thousand years, with culinary imprints ranging from the Saracens to the Normans. The heritage of many of Italy's most famous desserts, including *sorbetti*, *gelati*, and *semifreddi* (the most famous of which is probably tiramisu) dates back to the Saracen occupation of Sicily, which began in the early 800s. The origins of Cassata Siciliana go back to that time when Arabs were firmly installed in Palermo. The combination of flavors and the bright colors are typically Saracen. The word "cassata" comes from the Arabic *Quas'at*, which means "a large domed bowl" and describes the original shape of the cake. Many people confuse it with another dome-shaped Italian dessert, cassata gelato, an unmolded ice cream bombe that, like the Cassata Siciliana, contains maraschino-soaked candied fruit.

In its most basic form, Cassata Siciliana was simply a light pound or fruitcake (*pan di spagna*) layered with fresh ricotta and candied fruits. Originally, common additions included various nuts (especially pistachios and almonds), apricot jam, chocolate chunks, marzipan, and liqueur (most often maraschino), and the cake was usually iced with chocolate buttercream. As the years passed, the cake was decorated with green marzipan, citron, silvered chocolate balls, orange strips, decorative roses cut from church wafers, and multicolored whole candied fruits, often numerous and piled up in a somewhat inedible fashion atop the confection; the cake became a true baroque fantasy.

By the sixteenth century, Cassata Siciliana was commonly prepared by nuns in the convents and by cooks in Palermo's noble households. It became such a popular component of the Easter festivities that in 1575 the Church forbade its nuns from making it during Holy Week, expressing the sentiment that fussing with it was too big a distraction from religion. In time, the cake came to be popular at Christmas as well, and before long it was dragged out for almost all celebratory occasions.

The entire cassata can be assembled a day in advance and refrigerated. However, do not keep it too long, as very fresh ricotta is its identifying ingredient. If making the icing is too much work, simply frost with a thin layer of whipped cream and a sprinkling of chopped or shaved chocolate. Another attractive option is to use a piece of lace or a doily to stencil a cocoa pattern on the whipped cream, or just dust the cake itself with a bit of cocoa. However, there is the reward of authenticity plus oohs and aahs from your guests if you go all out with the chocolate icing and candied fruits.

Serves 10 to 12

2 pounds very fresh ricotta

3 tablespoons heavy cream

½ cup superfine sugar

5 tablespoons orange liqueur (such as Grand Marnier or Triple Sec) or rum

½ cup candied orange peel, cut into small dice

¼ cup candied lemon peel, cut into small dice

4 ounces semisweet chocolate, cut into small chunks

½ cup toasted pine nuts, coarsely chopped

1 Citrus-Scented Pound Cake (recipe follows), or good-quality store-bought pound cake

Chocolate Buttercream (recipe follows)

Toasted slivered almonds or pine nuts, or crumbled amaretti (optional)

1. Pass the ricotta through a food mill or force it through a coarse sieve or potato ricer into a mixing bowl. Beat it by hand or using an electric mixer until it is perfectly smooth.

2. Add the cream, sugar, and liqueur, and continue to beat. Using a rubber spatula, fold in the candied orange and lemon peels, chocolate, and pine nuts.

3. Lightly butter a 7½-by-4-inch charlotte mold or soufflé dish approximately the same size. Cut a circle of wax paper to fit in the bottom and a 4½-by-23-inch strip to line the sides (adjust size of wax paper for a soufflé dish). This will make it easy to unmold the cassata later.

4. Cut the pound cake into ½-inch slices. Line the prepared mold with cake, using whole slices for the sides and whole slices plus smaller pieces for the bottom, saving enough slices to cover the top. Use a sharp knife to trim the cake slices if they extend past the top of the mold.

5. Pour the ricotta mixture into the cake-lined mold and completely cover the ricotta with slices of cake. Cover with foil and refrigerate for at least 4 hours.

6. Turn the cassata out onto a cake plate. Ice with the Chocolate Buttercream. Refrigerate for at least 30 minutes, then serve. This can be done up to a day in advance, provided the ricotta is very fresh. Sprinkle with toasted slivered almonds or pine nuts, or crumbled amaretti, if desired.

CITRUS-SCENTED POUND CAKE

Makes 1 (9-by-5-inch) cake

2 cups sifted cake flour
1 teaspoon baking powder
¼ teaspoon salt
5 large eggs, at room temperature
1 teaspoon vanilla extract
½ teaspoon almond extract
Finely grated zest of ½ lemon
Finely grated zest of ½ orange
1 cup (2 sticks) unsalted butter, at room temperature
1⅓ cups sugar

1. Preheat the oven to 325 degrees. Butter and flour a 9-by-5-inch loaf pan. Line the bottom with parchment paper; butter the paper.
2. Sift the flour together with the baking powder and salt; set aside.
3. Whisk together the eggs, vanilla and almond extracts, and lemon and orange zests; set aside.
4. Using an electric mixer, cream the butter and sugar until light and fluffy, about 10 minutes, scraping down the sides of the bowl. While beating, slowly add the egg mixture. Beat again until light and fluffy, scraping down the sides of the bowl as necessary. Fold in the flour mixture in three parts using a rubber spatula or beat on low speed until just combined.
5. Scrape the batter into the prepared pan, smooth the top, and bake until a cake tester inserted in the center comes out clean, about 70 minutes. Let cool on a wire rack for 10 minutes, then turn the cake out of the pan and re-invert to let cool right side up.

CHOCOLATE BUTTERCREAM

4 ounces semisweet chocolate, coarsely chopped
3 large egg yolks
⅔ cup sugar
¼ teaspoon cream of tartar
10 tablespoons unsalted butter, cut into 1-inch pieces
1 tablespoon orange liqueur or rum (use the same liquor you use in the ricotta filling)

1. Place the chocolate and 2 tablespoons of water in the top of a double boiler or in a metal bowl set over a saucepan of simmering water. When the chocolate is melted, remove from the heat and set aside to cool.
2. Using an electric mixer, beat the egg yolks until light and thickened, about 5 minutes.
3. In a small saucepan, combine the sugar, cream of tartar, and 5 tablespoons water. Insert a candy thermometer in the pan and bring the mixture to a boil.
4. Start beating the egg yolks again, and, when the candy thermometer reads 236 degrees, immediately remove the pan from the heat and, continuing to beat, pour the hot syrup into the egg yolks in a slow, steady stream. Continue to beat at medium speed until *completely* cool, 10 to 15 minutes.
5. Beat in the butter pieces, one by one, incorporating well after each addition, then beat in the cooled chocolate, followed by the liqueur. If the mixture is too thin to spread, place it in the refrigerator until a spreading consistency is reached. If the icing separates, warm it a little bit over low heat and beat it again until smooth. Some fussing may be necessary at this point—warming, beating, refrigerating, beating—to achieve the proper consistency.

Note: Buttercream can be stored in the refrigerator for 3 to 4 days. It will keep in the freezer for much longer.

La Galette des Rois

Galettes have been around since the beginning of history. *Larousse Gastronomique* describes a galette as a "flat round cake of variable size [which] probably dates from the Neolithic era, when thick cereal pastes were cooked by spreading them out on hot stones." In the Middle Ages, with the arrival of the hearth, these stone-baked cakes made with various grains and flavored with honey were replaced by more refined regional varieties. Correz included walnuts or chestnuts; Roussillon used candied fruits; Jura, curd cheese; Normandy, puff pastry filled with jam and fresh cream. The most famous of these galettes is the Galette des Rois, eaten at Twelfth Night. In northern France this cake is similar to the puff pastry creation of Normandy, but is filled with almond cream, often with a little jam. In southern France the galette is brioche-based, perfumed with eau de vie or orange-flower water and studded with candied fruit.

Whatever the version, the defining feature of the cake is the fava bean hidden inside, a tradition that began in the Middle Ages when king's cake (*roi* is the French word for king) was first associated with Epiphany. Everyone hoped to find the bean in his slice, as it signified good luck for the year to come. As the years passed, coins and other charms, such as a porcelain or gold baby, moon, king, or leaf, were used instead of, or along with, the bean.

Legend has it that the cake was named for the Three Kings, Melchior, Gaspar, and Balthazar. Some say the galette represents gifts brought to the infant Jesus; some see it as a metaphor for a king's crown; others see its circular form as a symbol of the sun, much absent from the sky at the time this cake was eaten just a few weeks after the Winter Solstice.

What passes for king's cake in New Orleans is a different animal indeed: a braid of moist enriched yeast cake, decorated with garish green, purple, and yellow sugar crystals and containing as its treasure a bubblegum pink little plastic baby rather than a *fève*. Bakeries there feature these cakes in all shapes and sizes during Mardi Gras week. According to Louisiana tradition, the person "lucky" enough to find the baby on his plate must give the following year's Mardi Gras ball. Why this cake is eaten during Mardi Gras in New Orleans while in other places it is consumed on Twelfth Night, January 6, is a mystery to me.

Serves 10 to 12

1½ pounds puff pastry (best-quality store-bought)

For the pastry cream:
1 cup milk
Finely grated zest of 1 orange
Finely grated zest of 1 lemon
¼ cup sugar
Large pinch of salt
3 large egg yolks
3½ tablespoons all-purpose flour

For the almond paste:
7 tablespoons sugar
1 scant cup toasted blanched almonds
7 tablespoons unsalted butter, at room temperature
2 large eggs, at room temperature
2 tablespoons brandy
2½ tablespoons all-purpose flour

For assembling and baking the galette:
1 dried fava or lima bean
4 tablespoons apricot (or other) jam (optional)
1 large egg yolk, whisked with 1 tablespoon of
    heavy cream

1. On a lightly floured board, roll out the puff pastry a bit less than ⅛ inch thick. Keep turning the pastry over as you roll. If it becomes too elastic, let it rest for a few minutes, then continue.
2. Using a dinner plate, trace two 12-inch circles in the dough with the tip of a sharp knife and then cut them out. Place the rounds on a plate, separated by a piece of wax or parchment paper, and refrigerate.

To make the pastry cream:
1. Put the milk and zests in a small saucepan and bring to a boil.
2. Meanwhile, whisk the sugar, salt, egg yolks, and flour together in a medium-sized bowl.
3. As soon as the milk boils, pour it in a thin stream into the egg yolk mixture, whisking constantly.
4. Return the mixture to the saucepan and heat, stirring constantly. Boil gently for 2 minutes, stirring. The mixture should be very thick. Transfer it to a bowl and place a piece of plastic wrap directly on the surface to prevent a skin from forming. Let cool completely.

To make the almond paste:
1. Place the sugar and almonds in a food processor and process until very finely ground. Add the butter and pulse several times. Add the eggs and brandy and process to mix, then add the flour. Process until just combined.

To assemble and bake the galette:
1. Preheat the oven to 400 degrees.
2. When the pastry cream is completely cool, stir it together with the almond paste and bury the dried bean in it.
3. Remove the pastry circles from the refrigerator. Lay one on a parchment-lined baking sheet. Spread the jam (if using) evenly over the pastry, leaving a 1-inch border. Paint the border lightly with water.
4. Put the almond pastry cream on top of the jam and place the second pastry circle on top. Press the edges together well and crimp with a fork or pie crimper. Brush the top surface with the egg yolk–cream mixture and make a shallow crisscross pattern in the top with a sharp knife, but do not cut all the way through the pastry. Cut a slit in the middle to allow steam to escape.
5. Bake the galette in the lower third of the oven until golden, about 40 minutes. Serve warm. You can make the galette earlier in the day and reheat in a 350-degree oven for about 10 minutes.

THE TRIDENT'S

Carrot Cake

Back in the 1960s, anybody who was anybody hung out at Sausalito's Trident jazz club. Owned by the Kingston Trio, it was famous for its music, its scene, and its food, especially the moist, nutty carrot cake. Having French chef Pierre in the kitchen was a lucky break for the Trident. The then-assistant manager of the club, Carmen Robles, describes Pierre as "a truly interesting person and a colorful and inventive chef, way ahead of his time." He cooked a traditional French menu — *coquilles St. Jacques*, onion soup gratinée, coq au vin, sole meunière, duck à l'orange, and the like — each dish with his own special twist.

In 1967 the Trident closed for renovation and reopened later that year as, according to Robles, "the most elegant hippy club you've ever seen." In keeping with this new image, Pierre pursued more "healthy, vegetarian-type" dishes. It was at this time he was at his most creative, combining his French training with a California aesthetic. Enter the carrot cake.

In California in the late 1960s, carrot cake was a big deal, a necessary inclusion on the menu of the spiffy new Trident. Slices of the best carrot cakes from around the Bay Area were purchased for Pierre to taste and deconstruct. "What is this?" he asked. "I can make a better one!" And he did.

For many years Pierre kept his carrot cake recipe a secret, despite requests for it almost daily. Robles eventually left the Trident to manage Brebner Casting Agency, and at one point needed a "French chef" for a commercial. Naturally, she thought of Pierre, with his little black mustache and French-accented English. During the filming, Pierre and Robles became good friends, and again, she asked for the secret recipe; but Pierre continued to hold out. Finally, just before he died, she got what she wanted; he handed over the precious recipe. She passed it along to me, and I'm including it here as originally written.

Serves 12

For the carrot cake:
2⅓ cups tasteless vegetable oil such as canola
2⅔ cups sugar
6 large eggs, at room temperature
4 teaspoons vanilla extract
2 teaspoons ground cinnamon
2 teaspoons baking soda
1 teaspoon salt
3⅓ cups all-purpose flour, sifted
5⅓ cups finely grated carrots (two 1-pound bags peeled
    baby carrots grated in a food processor)
1⅓ cups finely chopped toasted walnuts
1⅓ cups raisins
1 (20-ounce) can crushed pineapple (about 1⅓ cups),
    well drained
1⅓ cups sweetened shredded coconut

For the cream cheese icing:
1 cup (2 sticks) unsalted butter, at room temperature
24 ounces cold cream cheese
2 tablespoons vanilla extract
7 cups confectioners' sugar, sifted
Pinch of salt
Grated zest of 1 orange or lemon

To make the carrot cake:
1. Preheat the oven to 325 degrees. Line the bottom of three 9- or 10-inch cake pans with parchment paper; butter the paper and flour the paper and the pans.
2. Using an electric mixer, beat the oil, sugar, eggs, vanilla, cinnamon, baking soda, and salt until very thoroughly combined.
3. Add the flour and stir just until the batter is smooth.
4. In a separate bowl, combine the carrots, walnuts, raisins, pineapple, and coconut. Add the batter and stir with a spatula until thoroughly combined.
5. Divide the batter evenly among the prepared pans.
6. Place in the preheated oven and bake until a cake tester inserted in the center comes out clean, about 1 hour and 15 minutes.
7. Let the cakes cool 15 minutes in their pans and then invert them onto wire racks to cool completely.

To make the cream cheese icing:
1. Process all of the ingredients in a food processor until just smooth and creamy. Do not overprocess. Or, use an electric mixer to cream the butter, cream cheese, vanilla, salt, and zest until just blended. Add the confectioners' sugar, one-third at a time, beating until smooth and a spreading consistency is reached.
2. Generously spread the icing between the layers and use the rest to ice the cake.

Crème Fraîche Cheesecake

Long ago, back in the days when truffle oil was not available at the corner deli and a hundred and one flavors of vodka did not exist; when there were no designer chocolates and no one had heard of aged "balsamico," there was Zausner crème fraîche.

In 1974 I was living in Cambridge near Harvard Square and had barely heard of crème fraîche, let alone seen it for sale. Even fancy and very upscale Sage's Market on Brattle Street did not carry it . . . until one day, it did. The brand was Santé, made by the Zausner Company in New Holland, Pennsylvania. I later learned that it was the only crème fraîche available anywhere in the United States at that time. Sol Zausner, a manufacturer of dairy products, introduced it in the United States, after being prodded to develop an American version by family members who took annual gastronomic tours of France.

When I saw it at Sage's, I had to buy some, even though I had no idea what to do with it. Luckily there was a small beige pamphlet taped to the container providing enlightenment: "This is your

recipe book," and then "for use in all cream sauces and as a topping for fruit, berries and dessert." I first tried it on berries and was an instant convert. There were also recipes for crème fraîche with chicken and mushrooms, crème fraîche in a rémoulade sauce, and crème fraîche in an asparagus flan. But I decided to try the cheesecake.

To this day, I adore Zausner's Crème Fraîche Cheesecake. It is crustless, light, fluffy, and not too sweet. A tall, homogeneous entity—there are no layers—it's delicious served with fresh fruit, berries, or a berry coulis; but, honestly, I prefer to savor each creamy bite with no distraction, not even coffee. Since it is not overly sweet, the cake goes well with a Sauternes-style dessert wine.

Serves 20

4 cups crème fraîche, at room temperature (you can sub-
    stitute sour cream if you must)
3 pounds cream cheese cut into small pieces, at room
    temperature
8 large eggs, at room temperature
1½ cups sugar
Finely grated zest of 1 large lemon
Finely grated zest of ½ orange
Juice of 1½ large lemons
2 tablespoons vanilla extract
2 tablespoons sifted all-purpose flour

1. Preheat the oven to 500 degrees. Generously butter a 10-inch springform pan.
2. Place half of the crème fraîche in the bowl of an electric mixer. Beat well, adding half of the cream cheese pieces one chunk or two at a time.
3. Beat in 2 of the eggs, one at a time.
4. Beat in the remaining crème fraîche and then the sugar.
5. Beat in the lemon and orange zests and lemon juice.
6. Beat in the rest of the cream cheese, a chunk or two at a time.
7. Add the vanilla, then the flour, and then the remaining 6 eggs, one at a time, and beat until completely smooth.

8. Pour the batter into the prepared pan and bake in the lower third of the oven for 10 minutes. Lower the oven temperature to 275 degrees and keep the oven door open for 5 minutes so it will cool down quickly. Close the oven door and bake until done, about 1½ to 2 hours more. The top will be golden, the cake will rise about 1½ inches, and a cake tester inserted in the center will come out clean.
9. Let cool on a rack for 1 hour, then remove the sides of the springform pan and let cool for 3 hours more. Cover and refrigerate. This cake is best made a day ahead.

Notes: An approximation of Zausner's crème fraîche can be made by stirring 2 to 3 tablespoons of plain yogurt or buttermilk into 4 cups of heavy cream. Leave the mixture at room temperature, partly covered, until it thickens; stir occasionally. It can take up to two or three days to thicken. Once thick, cover and refrigerate; it will keep up to a month.

To make a smaller cake to serve 10, halve the recipe and use an 8-inch springform pan. Proceed with the recipe but bake the cake only 1 hour to 1 hour and 20 minutes once you have lowered the oven temperature.

Chocolate Pastry Cake

When thinking about favorite restaurants that no longer exist, Tower Suite, La Fonda del Sol, Forum of the Twelve Caesars, the Hawaiian Room, and Windows on the World all come to mind. These restaurants—as well as New York's Four Seasons, which is still thriving—were owned and operated by Restaurant Associates. In their book *The Four Seasons: America's Premier Restaurant*, John Mariani and Alex von Bidder remember RA in its heyday as "a gaggle of young, enthusiastic men who produced some of the grandest and some of the most contrived restaurants of the era"—an era that was ready for dining as theater, stage set, and spectacle.

Originally, Restaurant Associates was the business name of the Riker's coffee shop chain acquired in 1942 by Abraham Wecksler. RA also ran a hotdog stand in the old Newark, New Jersey, airport. It was so successful with its foot-long fifteen-cent hotdogs that when the airport was rebuilt in 1952, the Port Authority asked Wecksler to open a luxury restaurant in the same location. He hired the thirty-something Joe Baum to oversee the project, and the rest is history. Baum was a showman. In *On the Town in New York,* Ariane and Michael Batterberry state that he turned the Newarker into "the proverbial three-ringed circus. Oysters were served by the sevens, lobsters had three claws, and everything was flambé"—even steak and shashlik. Against all odds (an expensive restaurant in a busy commuter airport in the 1950s—and in Newark!), the restaurant was a huge success and others soon followed, one more imaginative, distinctive, and eccentric than the next. Most had regional or historic themes. The Batterberry's note that each one was "a packaged masterpiece . . . a cross between an 'on location' MGM costume epic production and a State Department study of underdeveloped areas." According to restaurateur George Lang, who joined RA in 1960 and is associated with it to this day, a mind-boggling amount of research went into creating each restaurant. Although it is difficult to imagine, when La Brasserie opened in 1959 the word "brasserie" was all but unknown in New York, and when La Fonda del Sol opened a few years later, it was the first restaurant in the United States to serve guacamole. Most importantly, though, RA merged big business and revolution—breaking away from the accepted traditions of restaurant design, service, and menus, to permanently change the way New Yorkers (and eventually the entire nation) would view the experience of dining out.

Windows on the World was an elegant fifty-thousand-square-foot restaurant in the sky that opened in 1976 on top of the north tower of the World Trade Center. It existed until the events of 9/11. A meal at Windows was automatically an occasion. There was the trip downtown followed by the trip to the 107th floor, where patrons were greeted by a beautiful dining room, spectacular food and service, and, of course, those seemingly endless views of the Hudson River, New Jersey, Staten Island, and Lower Manhattan.

The brilliant Albert Kumin, who before helping to open Windows was head pastry chef and chocolatier at the Four Seasons, created the superlative Chocolate Pastry Cake. The distinguishing feature of this signature dish was the unexpected layering of crisp chocolate pastry alternating with Grand Marnier–soaked genoise and ganache—a delicious and unique combination. Neither too wet nor too sweet, the cake is even better accompanied by a scoop of coffee or vanilla ice cream.

Nick Malgieri, a pastry chef, cookbook author, and teacher, told me he "made the prototype cake with chef Kumin in early March 1976, before the Windows opening" and that the Chocolate Pastry Cake in his cookbook *How to Bake* is essentially Kumin's. The following recipe is an adaptation of Malgieri's.

Serves 12

For the chocolate genoise:
⅓ cup cake flour
⅓ cup cornstarch
¼ cup best-quality unsweetened nonalkalized
   cocoa powder
Large pinch of baking soda
3 large eggs, plus 3 yolks, at room temperature
¾ cup sugar
Pinch of salt

For the chocolate pastry:
3 cups all-purpose flour
½ cup best-quality nonalkalized unsweetened
   cocoa powder
⅓ cup sugar
¼ teaspoon baking soda
Pinch of salt
¾ pound (3 sticks) cold unsalted butter, cut into small
   pieces and kept refrigerated until ready to use

For the orange liqueur syrup:
⅔ cup sugar
⅓ cup orange liqueur (such as Grand Marnier or
   Triple Sec)

For the ganache:
1½ cups heavy cream
6 tablespoons unsalted butter
1¼ pounds semisweet chocolate, cut into small pieces

To make the chocolate genoise:
1. Preheat the oven to 350 degrees. Butter and flour a 9-inch round cake pan and line the bottom with parchment paper; butter the paper.
2. Stir together the cake flour, cornstarch, cocoa powder, and baking soda to combine well. Sift once and set aside.
3. Using an electric mixer, beat the eggs and egg yolks together. Add the sugar in a stream, beating constantly, and then add the salt.

4. Place the bowl with the egg mixture over a saucepan of simmering water and whisk until the mixture is lukewarm, about 1 minute.

5. Return to the mixer and beat on high speed for about 5 minutes, until the mixture has cooled to room temperature, lightened, and forms a ribbon when poured from a spoon.

6. Sift the dry ingredients into the egg mixture in three additions, folding after each addition with a rubber spatula.

7. Pour the batter into the prepared pan and bake in the center of the oven for 25 to 30 minutes, until a cake tester inserted in the center comes out clean.

8. Let cool for 10 minutes, then run a knife around the sides and invert the cake onto a wire rack. Immediately re-invert and let the cake cool completely.

To make the chocolate pastry:

1. Combine the flour, cocoa powder, sugar, baking soda, and salt in the bowl of a food processor.

2. Add the butter and pulse until the butter bits are the size of small peas.

3. With the motor running, add 4 tablespoons ice water all at once and pulse until the mixture just begins to come together. You may need to add more water at this point, but add only a tiny bit at a time, enough so that the dough just holds together.

4. Remove the dough from the food processor and divide it into four equal parts. Form each part into a ball and flatten each ball into a disk.

5. Using a rolling pin, roll each disk between two pieces of parchment paper to a thickness of about ³⁄₁₆ inch. Prick each piece of dough many times with a fork.

6. Pile the pieces of rolled dough, between their papers, on top of each other and refrigerate for at least 2 hours or up to 2 days (the dough can be well wrapped in aluminum foil at this point and frozen for 2 months).

7. When ready to bake, preheat the oven to 325 degrees. Place oven racks in the lower and middle parts of the oven. Place each piece of dough on its paper on a baking sheet large enough to hold it, place a second baking sheet on top of each piece of dough, and bake until the layers are dry and crisp, about 30 minutes. Bake in several batches, if necessary.

8. Transfer the pastry pieces to a cutting board and cut each piece while still warm into a 9-inch circle. Let cool. Crumble the trimmings and set aside.

To make the orange liqueur syrup:

1. Combine the sugar and ¹⁄₃ cup water in a small saucepan and bring to a boil; boil until the sugar has dissolved then remove from the heat. When cool, stir in the orange liqueur.

To make the ganache:

1. Bring the cream and butter to a boil in a medium saucepan. Remove from the heat, add the chocolate, and let the mixture stand for 2 minutes. Whisk until smooth. Let cool.

To assemble the cake:

1. Using an electric mixer, beat the cooled ganache on medium speed until light and smooth, 1 to 2 minutes, scraping down the sides of the bowl two or three times with a rubber spatula.

2. Split the genoise into 3 equal layers and paint the top of each layer with one third of the syrup.

3. Place a chocolate pastry layer on a serving plate or piece of cardboard. Spread a layer of ganache about ³⁄₈ inch thick on the pastry and then top that with a layer of genoise, then another layer of pastry, ganache, and genoise; continue layering, ending with a pastry layer on top.

4. Ice the top and sides of the cake with the remaining ganache and press the pastry crumbs into the ganache around the sides and on top of the cake.

5. Keep the cake at room temperature until ready to serve, but no more than 24 hours. Well-wrapped leftovers will keep refrigerated for up to 1 week or for several months frozen.

Note: The chocolate pastry is very fragile. If it breaks (and it probably will), just piece it together and use it anyway. No one will notice.

SCANDIA'S

Princess Cake

In the 1950s, Uncle John from Stockholm introduced my parents and me to the original Scandia on Sunset Boulevard in Beverly Hills. It was opened in 1946 by Kenneth Hansen and his sister Teddy, emigrants from Copenhagen, who arrived and soon knew everyone in town. By the time the restaurant moved across the street ten years later, it had become a watering hole for the who's who of Hollywood. Errol Flynn, Victor Borge, and Everett Crosby, Bing's brother and manager, all members of the Viking Club, met there on a regular basis. Teddy was in charge of the wood-paneled dining room, the tables set with crystal glassware and blue and white Royal Copenhagen china. The principal decorations were huge hanging antique copper pots and oversized coats of arms that lined the walls.

People flocked to Scandia for one of the first true Scandinavian smorgasbords in America and for "the Oskar," a rich veal dish sauced with béarnaise and garnished with crab legs and asparagus. But my love affair was with the Princess Cake and its wonderful marzipan. For me, this splendid multilayered cake was the high point of every dinner at Scandia. Combining chocolate icing, marzipan, buttercream, rum, almond macaroons, and raspberry jam, it's everything I love in dessert. The plethora of components makes this cake a bit of a hassle to prepare, but it's well worth the trouble. A silver lining is that virtually all of the parts can be made up to several days ahead, and the entire thing put together the day before serving. I have tasted similar Danish cakes in various pastry shops around the world, but my favorite is still Scandia's.

Serves 8 to 10

For the yellow cakes:
3 large egg yolks
½ cup milk
1¼ teaspoons vanilla extract
1½ cups sifted cake flour
¾ cup sugar
2 teaspoons baking powder
⅜ teaspoon salt
6 tablespoons unsalted butter, at room temperature

For the vanilla buttercream: (This may be more buttercream than you need. If so, the extra freezes well.)
3 large egg yolks
6 tablespoons sugar
¼ cup light corn syrup
1 cup (2 sticks) unsalted butter, softened
4 teaspoons vanilla extract

For the marzipan icing:
1 cup almond paste
1 cup confectioners' sugar, sifted
1 large egg plus one egg yolk (or a bit more if needed
   to make a spreading consistency)
½ teaspoon vanilla extract

For the chocolate icing:
2 ounces unsweetened chocolate, cut into small pieces
½ cup confectioners' sugar, sifted
1 tablespoon hot water
1 large egg, at room temperature and lightly beaten
3 tablespoons unsalted butter, at room temperature

To assemble the cake:
24 bakery-bought almond macaroons—somewhat soft
   and chewy, not hard and crisp
About 5 tablespoons dark rum
About 2 cups best-quality raspberry jam

To make the yellow cakes:
1. Preheat the oven to 350 degrees. Butter two 6- or 8-inch round or square cake pans at least 1½ inches deep. Line the bottoms with parchment paper; butter the paper and dust the paper and pans with flour.
2. In a mixing bowl, combine the egg yolks, 2 tablespoons of the milk, and the vanilla.
3. Place the flour, sugar, baking powder, and salt in the bowl of an electric mixer and mix for 30 seconds until combined. Add the butter and the remaining 6 tablespoons milk. Mix on low speed until uniformly moist. Switch to high speed and mix for 1½ minutes. Add the egg mixture in three batches, beating 15 seconds after each addition and scraping down the sides of the bowl with a rubber spatula.
4. Divide the batter evenly between the prepared pans and smooth the surfaces with a spatula. Bake until a cake tester inserted near the center comes out clean and the cake springs back when pressed lightly in the center, 20 to 25 minutes. The cakes should start to shrink from the sides of the pan only after they are removed from the oven.
5. Cool on wire racks for 10 minutes, then loosen the cakes from the sides of the pan with a small knife and invert the cakes onto the racks. Re-invert and cool completely.
6. Split each cake horizontally into two layers.

To make the vanilla buttercream:
1. Using an electric mixer, beat the egg yolks until light and fluffy, about 5 minutes.
2. Meanwhile combine the sugar and corn syrup in a small saucepan and cook, stirring constantly, until the syrup comes to a rolling boil and the sugar dissolves, and the entire surface is covered with large bubbles. Immediately pour the syrup into another cool saucepan or metal bowl to stop the cooking.
3. Beating constantly, add the syrup to the egg yolks in a slow, steady stream. Use a rubber spatula to scrape the last of the syrup into the yolks and to scrape down the bowl occasionally. Continue to beat until the mixture is completely cool.
4. Gradually beat in the butter and then the vanilla. Store the buttercream in an airtight container in the refrigerator. Bring to room temperature and beat again before using.

To make the marzipan icing:

1. Cut the almond paste into small pieces and place in the bowl of an electric mixer with the sugar, the whole egg, and the egg yolk. Beat on medium speed until combined, adding more egg if necessary to make the icing a spreading consistency. Add the vanilla and beat until combined.

To make the chocolate icing:

1. Melt the chocolate in the top of a double boiler or a metal bowl set over a saucepan of simmering water. When melted, remove from the heat and add the confectioners' sugar and hot water. Stir thoroughly. Add the egg and beat well. Add the butter 1 tablespoon at a time and beat until thoroughly combined, smooth, and glossy.

To assemble the cake:

1. Lay the macaroons out on a piece of wax paper, flatten them a bit with your hand, and sprinkle with 2 tablespoons of the rum. Set aside.

2. Lay a cake layer on a cake plate and dampen the top with 1 tablespoon of the rum. Spread generously with jam and then cover evenly with 12 of the macaroons.

3. Spread the underside of a second cake layer with buttercream, about 3/8 inch thick. Place this second layer, buttercream side down, on top of the first layer. Dampen the top with 1 tablespoon of rum.

4. Spread the top of this second layer generously with jam.

5. Spread the underside of a third cake layer with buttercream, again about 3/8 inch thick, and lay it, buttercream side down, on top of the second layer.

6. Dampen the top of the third layer with the last tablespoon of the rum, spread generously with jam, and evenly cover the jam with the remaining 12 macaroons.

7. Spread 3/8 inch of buttercream on the underside of the fourth cake layer and lay it, buttercream side down, on top of the third layer.

8. Use leftover buttercream sparingly to tidy up the cake: fill gaps on the sides between layers and generally smooth things over. Put the cake in the refrigerator or freezer for at least 15 minutes to harden the buttercream.

9. When the buttercream is hard, ice the cake with a layer of marzipan icing. Refrigerate or freeze for about 15 minutes, again to harden the icing, and then ice a final time with the chocolate icing.

10. The cake should be kept in the refrigerator until one hour before serving. It can be assembled up to 24 hours in advance and kept well covered and refrigerated. It can also be frozen.

Note: The vanilla buttercream, the marzipan, and the chocolate icing will keep in the refrigerator for several days. To store longer, freeze.

GEORGE LANG'S

Dobos Torte

I always adored my Aunt Iva's Dobos Torte, which was really the *Gourmet Cookbook*'s Dobos Torte. I loved the cake for its many layers, which resulted in a wonderful, over-the-top excess of chocolate buttercream. Above all, I adored the mystery of the thick, glassy hard-caramel top. It is the only cake I know that has this feature. The caramel crunches and crackles with every bite.

Jozsef C. Dobos has been described as the "Escoffier of Hungary." Dobos's career more or less coincided with that of Escoffier and, like him, Dobos's name and his recipes became known far beyond his country's borders. Dobos opened a food specialty shop in Budapest that was unique at the time. In an age when shipping was expensive and unreliable, he stocked more than sixty kinds of cheese and twenty-two varieties of Champagne, and procured from all over every rare seasonal delicacy imaginable. It was in this shop in 1887 that he created the Dobos Torte and devised a packaging system to ship his cake around the world. The cake was so popular that the Millennium Exposition in 1896 had a Dobos Pavilion that carried nothing but these cakes. Thousands of them were sold, resulting in serious Dobosmania. This popularity resulted from the cake's extravagance of buttercream, unusual at a time when most cakes were filled with whipped cream, pastry cream, or custard. Though imitated constantly, with consistently bad results, the real recipe remained a secret until 1906, when Dobos donated it to the Hungarian Pastry and Honey-Bread Makers Guild.

Who could be a better source of the authentic Dobos Torte recipe than George Lang, the brilliant restaurateur of Hungarian descent? Lang is the owner of New York City's beautiful landmark Café des Artistes, and an author. His books include the charming and amusing *George Lang's Compendium of Culinary Nonsense and Trivia*, his spellbinding autobiography, *Nobody Knows the Truffles I've Seen*, and the definitive cookbook, *George Lang's The Cuisine of Hungary*.

Dobos died in 1924, the year George Lang was born. Lang wistfully told me he often hoped his skills were a reincarnation of the master's culinary talents. I, for one, am sure they are.

Serves 12

For the cakes:
10 large eggs, separated, at room temperature
⅛ teaspoon salt
½ teaspoon cream of tartar
1 cup plus ⅔ cup sugar
1 cup pastry flour, or ½ cup all-purpose flour combined
     with ½ cup cake flour
Chocolate Filling (recipe follows)

1. Preheat the oven to 375 degrees. Butter and flour three 9-inch round cake pans. Line the bottom of each with wax or parchment paper; butter the paper.
2. Using an electric mixer fitted with the whisk attachment, beat the egg whites, salt, and cream of tartar until soft peaks form.
3. Add the egg yolks, two at a time, beating 30 seconds after each addition.
4. Turn the mixer to its slowest speed and very gradually, so as not to deflate the batter, add 1 cup sugar.
5. Very gradually add the flour until just combined.
6. Divide the batter in half and divide one half equally among the 3 prepared pans. Set the other half aside. Tap each filled pan hard on the counter to remove air bubbles and even out the batter. Bake in the middle of the oven for 10 to 12 minutes, until golden around the edges and a cake tester inserted in the center comes out clean. Let the cake layers cool for 5 minutes, then invert them onto a wire rack to cool. Remove the paper circles. Wash and prepare the pans and repeat the process with the remaining half of the batter (if you happen to have six pans, you can bake all six layers at once). Cover the baked cake layers lightly with kitchen towels while they cool to keep them moist.
7. Set the most attractive cake layer aside to use for the top of the cake. Place it on a piece of buttered aluminum foil.
8. Place one of the remaining five layers on a serving plate. Spread it with a layer of chocolate filling about ³⁄₁₆ inch thick. Place another of the cake layers on top and repeat until all five cake layers are used, ending with a layer of filling. Set the remaining filling aside.
9. Make the hard caramel for the top of the cake: In a small saucepan over medium heat, combine the remaining ⅔ cup sugar and ⅓ cup water. Stir until the syrup boils and becomes clear, then stop stirring. When the

caramel is a deep caramel color, 370 degrees on a candy thermometer, remove it from the heat. As soon as it stops bubbling, immediately pour it onto the cake layer you have set aside, pouring carefully so the entire top is evenly covered. Do not worry if some of the caramel runs off the cake onto the foil. Very quickly, before the caramel hardens (it will harden in less than a minute), score it into 12 wedge-shaped portions with the tip of a sharp buttered knife, then cut all the way through the scoring. During this process be careful not to touch the hot caramel with your fingers.
10. When the caramel is cool, put the scored caramel-covered layer on top of the cake. Put the remaining chocolate filling in a pastry tube fitted with a no. 6 tip and pipe a decorative border around the top edge of the torte, or just use a knife or small spatula to frost over any spots of cake that may still be showing around the top edge of the torte.
11. Place the torte, covered, in the refrigerator until the filling is firm, at least 4 hours and up to 4 days.
12. When ready to serve, cut into 12 wedges with a sharp knife dipped in hot water.

Chocolate filling:
1 vanilla bean
1½ cups confectioners' sugar
12 ounces (3 sticks) unsalted butter, at room temperature
Pinch of salt
6 tablespoons strong coffee
2 eggs, at room temperature
6 ounces semisweet chocolate, chopped

1. Split the vanilla bean and scrape the seeds into the sugar. Using an electric mixer, cream the vanilla sugar with the butter until well blended. Add the salt, coffee, and eggs, and mix until light and fluffy, about 5 to 10 minutes, scraping down the sides of the bowl frequently with a rubber spatula.
2. In the top of a double boiler or in a metal bowl set over a saucepan of simmering water, melt the chocolate. Cool to lukewarm and beat it into the butter-egg mixture.
3. Place in the refrigerator for 15 minutes to harden up a bit before using. You can make the filling ahead. If it is too hard, bring to room temperature or heat slightly and rebeat to bring to a spreading consistency.

Neapolitan Cake

"More care of cleanliness and attractiveness should be taken of the kitchen than of the reception-room."

"Everything in the kitchen should be spick and span, that is elementary. But what is not elementary is this: *Never cook in enameled vessels.* All cooking produces tartaric acid to a greater and lesser degree, and this attacks the enamel, producing tartar emetic, which is poison. So now you know."

These opening paragraphs of the Vicomte de Mauduit's cookbook, *The Vicomte in the Kitchen* (1933), are neither charming nor auspicious. The same can be said of the book's long and pretentious subtitle: "The Art of Cooking, Preserving, Eating, and Drinking; with the manner how to make simple dishes; all kinds of Banqueting Stuffs: of the Wines to be drunk with them: and of Sauces, Syrups, and Jam. Also a selection of Recipes from many Continents, Countries, and Counties; together with many economic and Distinguished Novelties; with finally a choice of Menus for all Occasions, Seasons, Purses, and Moods."

However, Vicomte Georges de Mauduit de Kervern's cookbook, despite its bad start, goes on to be informative, authoritative, and witty. In the preface to the first edition, Frances, Countess of Warwick, refers to the spectacular ingredients but mediocre food available in England at the time, stating "God sends the food, and the Devil, the cooks." She is clearly implying that God sent the Vicomte de Mauduit and his four cookbooks to England to culinarily elevate the English-speaking world.

A true delight to read and to cook from, the book was a bestseller, receiving scores of rave reviews. The *Daily Telegraph* read, "this lovable and erudite Frenchman, whose family goes back

to William the Conqueror, has known famous cooks all over the world, and been permitted to enter and ravish the secrets of their kitchens. His gastronomic Odyssey . . . is the succulently successful result of such ravishings." The *Edinburgh Evening News* called the vicomte "Mrs. Beeton's most worthy successor . . . she has not only been succeeded but excelled by a French nobleman."

The author was born in 1893 into an aristocratic French family. He went to school in England and then traveled extensively; the subtitle of his autobiographical *Private Views* (1932) is *Reminiscences of a Wandering Nobleman*. He lived in England, France, and America, had well-connected friends around the world, and was an accomplished adventurer who, in addition to cooking and writing, worked on irrigation projects in Egypt and was an aviator in World War II. About his culinary passions, he notes in his preface to *The Vicomte in the Kitchen* that while "I have spent, like most people, at least one third of my life in bed, it is of equal veracity to claim that I have spent at least one sixth of my life in the kitchen or among matters pertaining to the kitchen."

Chapter Ten of *The Vicomte in the Kitchen*, "Of Sweets, Puddings, Cakes and Confections," opens with a quote from a Shakespearean sonnet: "and Sweets grown common lose their dear delight." There certainly are some far-from-common desserts in the vicomte's book including vermicelli pudding; an Algerian roll made with dates and almonds; rose mousse; a raspberry Haslemere; Eggedosis, a Norweigan Easter treat; and "cambrosia." Another unusual dessert, the vicomte's Naples cake, consists of a stack of six citrus and almond shortbread cookies each about eight inches in diameter; jam is spread between them and the whole is topped with more jam and then chopped almonds. Reminiscent of jam-filled cookies, it goes well with a bit of ice cream or crème anglaise, and is especially good in the late afternoon with a cup of tea.

The Duchess of Devonshire's excellent *Chatsworth Cookery Book* (1988) is the only place I came across another recipe for this cake. She calls it a Neapolitan Cake, essentially the same dessert with a slightly different name. The youngest of the six legendary Mitford sisters, the duchess found the instructions for this cake in her mother's "old receipt book." Given the popularity of the vicomte's recipes among the British upper classes in the 1930s and 1940s, it seems clear where Mrs. Mitford (Sydney Bowles, the baroness of Redesdale) found the recipe. Her daughter quotes her saying that the cake could be "eaten straightaway, but it is best after a couple of days when the jam has softened the biscuit, making it moist and easier to cut."

The vicomte likes using multiple types of jam alternating with custard, while the duchess calls for apricot preserves. If you have the time and inclination, make the Caramelized Fig and Raspberry Jam (the recipe follows). It is excellent in the cake and is also perfect at breakfast on toast or thinned with a bit of Kirsch or maraschino and used to sauce vanilla ice cream. Serve Neapolitan Cake plain or accompanied by créme anglaise, whipped cream, clotted cream, or vanilla ice cream on the side.

Serves 6 to 8

1 cup whole blanched almonds, toasted
3 cups all-purpose flour, sifted
1 cup (2 sticks) unsalted butter, at room temperature
1 cup sugar
¼ teaspoon salt
Finely grated zest of 1 lemon
Finely grated zest of 1 orange
4 large egg yolks, at room temperature
½ teaspoon almond extract
1 teaspoon orange-flower water
1 to 1½ cups Carmelized and Vanilla-scented Fig and
    Raspberry Jam (recipe follows), or good-quality
    store-bought jam of your choice (apricot, raspberry,
    strawberry, or peach)
⅓ cup coarsely chopped toasted blanched almonds

1. In a food processor, pulverize the 1 cup blanched almonds together with 2 tablespoons of the flour and set aside.
2. Using an electric mixer, cream the butter, sugar, salt, and lemon and orange zests until light and fluffy, scraping down the bowl frequently with a rubber spatula, about 5 minutes. Add the ground almonds and beat until well blended. Add the egg yolks, one at a time, beating after each addition, and then add the almond extract and orange-flower water. Add the remaining flour (3 cups minus the 2 tablespoons) and beat until well combined.
3. Divide the dough into 6 equal balls, using a scale if necessary.
4. Press each ball into a 7- or an 8-inch circle. (Use a plate as a guide or the bottom of a small cake or pie pan. The easiest method is to press each ball of dough into a circle inside a 7- or an 8-inch flan ring.) Transfer the dough circles, to parchment-lined baking sheets. Place the baking sheets in the refrigerator or freezer for at least 2 hours.
5. Preheat the oven to 375 degrees and bake the dough circles for about 15 minutes, or until light gold. Remove from the oven and cool completely on wire racks.
6. Lay one circle in the center of a serving plate. Spread with 3 to 4 tablespoons jam. Continue to layer the circles, spreading jam between each. Spread a thin layer of jam on the very top and cover that evenly with the chopped almonds. The cake can be served immediately, but it tastes better, and is easier to cut, if tightly wrapped and left for 2 to 3 days before serving.

CARAMELIZED AND VANILLA-SCENTED FIG AND RASPBERRY JAM

Makes about one quart

1¼ pounds sugar
½ vanilla bean, split and scraped
18 large, very ripe figs (overripe is even better), cut into
    eighths
4 (10 ounce) bags frozen raspberries, or 2½ pounds
    fresh raspberries
2 lavender flowers or 1 teaspoon dried lavender (optional)
Large pinch of salt
Grated zest of one lemon
Juice of 1 lemon (optional)
Pernod or Luxardo maraschino liqueur to taste (optional)

1. Place the sugar and ½ cup water in a saucepan, along with the scraped vanilla bean and its seeds. Cook, stirring, until the syrup is a deep, dark caramel.
2. Add the figs, raspberries, lavender, salt, and zest. Bring to a boil and simmer for 10 minutes.
3. Let cool to lukewarm, then add the lemon juice and liqueur to taste, if using.
4. Use immediately or store in the refrigerator for several months.

FROZEN DESSERTS

Vaux-le-Vicomte's Fané

Henri Soulé's Bombe Pavillon

Bananas Foster

Romanoff's Baked Alaska

Auguste Escoffier's Peach Melba

Antonin Carême's Nectarine Plombière

C. C. Brown's Hot Fudge Sundae

Antonin Carême's Strawberries Romanoff

The Zodiac Room's Toasted Pecan Balls

Brown Bread Ice Cream

Schrafft's Famous Butterscotch Sundae

Schrafft's Coffee Milkshake

Trader Vic's Flaming Tahitian Ice Cream

VAUX-LE-VICOMTE'S

Fané

The recipe for Cristina de Vogüé's Fané is truly lost—or maybe it never existed except in my sometimes-too-vivid imagination. Nonetheless, ever since I tasted it, Fané has been my favorite dessert of all time.

In 1980 I met Boulie (Marie Nugent-Head), who had just moved to New York to become director of development for the New York City Ballet. I had been urged to contact her by my dear friend, the late Julia Thorne. I called Boulie; we became fast friends and still are to this day.

A completely unexpected perk of this friendship was being invited in 2001 to stay at the legendary chateau of Vaux-le-Vicomte for New Year's Eve and the few days surrounding it. Boulie's first cousin, Cristina, and her husband, Patrice, Le Comte and Comtesse de Vogüé, own and are permanent residents of the magical chateau and gardens, created in the 1650s by the architect Louis Le Vau, the designer Charles Le Brun, and the landscape architect André Le Nôtre for Fouquet, finance minister to Louis XIV (the same trio would later build Versailles, modeling it on Vaux).

The food was fabulous. Luzia, Cristina's magnificent longtime cook, produced one amazing dish after another: a special egg pasta laden with black truffles and foie gras; a whole poached salmon smothered in half a kilo of osetra; more osetra served on toast points before every meal; the combination of green salad with a perfectly ripened creamy Vacheron, the best I've ever tasted; velvety pumpkin soup garnished with thinly sliced raw scallops and their roe, accompanied by a 1985

Baron de L Pouilly Fumé; and a lunch featuring the unusual but excellent pairing of leg of lamb and barley with a dried fruit compote—again with the perfectly chosen wine, a 1988 Lynch Bage.

But the highlights were the desserts: poached cherries with whipped cream *and* crème fraîche; flourless chocolate cake baked in a bain marie and served with more crème fraîche; a rich, buttercream dacquoise; various meringue concoctions often incorporating one flavor or another of the chateau's incomparable homemade ice cream, and usually accompanied by Luzia's perfect chocolate sauce. And then there was the Fané.

Fané means "faded" in French, and certainly this dessert has faded from everyone's memory but mine. New Year's Eve dinner began appropriately with another kilo of osetra and much vodka (tipping the culinary hat to the Russian branch of Cristina's family) and ended with the most delicious dessert I have ever tasted. When questioned, Cristina told me the dish was called Fané and described the recipe to me—a luscious combination of vanilla ice cream, whipped cream, meringue, white nougat, and shaved chocolate, the whole even better than the perfect parts—while I took notes.

However, at this point the story gets confusing. When I emailed Cristina a couple of years later to make sure I had the recipe and the facts straight, she wrote back saying she could not remember "this special cake"; even the word Fané rang no bells. She suggested two recipe possibilities, but neither suggestion resembled what I had actually tasted at Vaux, nor my notes. However, her curiosity now piqued, she asked me to send her *my* Fané recipe. I did, Luzia made it for Patrice, who adored it, and Cristina is now using it in a cookbook she is writing on Vaux desserts!

Serves 10 to 12

3 pints vanilla ice cream, best-quality store-bought
    or homemade (see recipe, page 190)
1½ bars white nougat (recipe follows) or 1 pound store-
    bought white nougat, chopped into ¼-inch pieces
1 recipe whipped cream
1 recipe meringue, broken into bite-sized pieces
    (recipe follows)
1 cup shaved bittersweet chocolate

For the white nougat (can be made weeks in advance):
Rice paper
1½ cups vanilla sugar (see recipe, page 191); regular
    sugar can be substituted
1½ teaspoons orange-flower water
⅔ cup mild honey, such as lavender, orange blossom,
    or wildflower
3 large egg whites, at room temperature

Large pinch of salt
1¼ teaspoons cream of tartar
2 cups blanched almonds, toasted and kept warm
1 cup hazelnuts, toasted and skinned, and/or
    toasted pistachios

For the meringue (can be made a week in advance):
3 large egg whites, at room temperature
Pinch of salt
¼ teaspoon cream of tartar
¾ cup superfine sugar

For the whipped cream:
5 cups very cold heavy cream
5 tablespoons superfine sugar
1½ teaspoons vanilla extract

To make the white nougat:

1. Butter the bottom and sides of a 10-inch square pan and line with the rice paper, letting the paper come up 1 to 2 inches higher than the sides.

2. Put the vanilla sugar, the orange-flower water, and $\frac{1}{2}$ cup water in a medium-sized saucepan over medium heat. Stir until the mixture boils and becomes clear, then stir in the honey and insert a candy thermometer in the saucepan.

3. Meanwhile, using an electric mixer fitted with the whisk attachment, beat the egg whites, salt, and cream of tartar on medium speed until the egg whites are very stiff, raising the speed to high as they begin to stiffen.

4. As soon as the sugar mixture reaches 302 degrees (the hard-crack stage) turn the mixer back to high and imme- diately add the hot sugar mixture in a slow, steady stream to the egg whites.

5. Beat on high speed for 10 minutes, scraping down the bowl occasionally. Put the bowl in a heavy skillet (to keep the mixture from burning) over low heat. Heat, stirring with a spatula or wooden spoon, until the mixture is slightly warm and just pliable.

6. Stir in the nuts, then spread the warm nougat into the prepared pan. Cover with more rice paper, cut to fit, and fold the edges down over the nougat to form a package. Place another, slightly smaller square pan on top of the nougat and weigh it down with heavy cans for at least 12 hours.

7. Unmold the nougat and cut it into five 2-by-10-inch bars. Cover the cut sides with more rice paper, cut to fit.

8. If the nougat seems very soft and does not hold its shape easily, place the bars on a baking sheet in a very low oven and let dry for up to several hours. Cool.

To make the whipped cream:

1. Using an electric mixer fitted with the whisk attach- ment, whip the cream. When it begins to thicken, add the superfine sugar and vanilla, and continue to beat until the cream forms soft peaks.

2. Place 2 cups of the whipped cream in a seperate con- tainer in the refrigerator. This will be used later to ice the unmolded dessert.

To make the meringue:

1. Preheat the oven to 200 degrees. Line a baking sheet with parchment paper.

2. Using an electric mixer fitted with the whisk attachment, beat the egg whites together with the salt and the cream of tartar on low speed. Slowly raise the speed as the whites turn opaque and soft peaks form.

3. Add the superfine sugar, 1 tablespoon at a time, until the meringue holds stiff peaks.

4. Spread the meringue into a $1\frac{1}{2}$-inch-thick layer on the parchment-lined baking sheet. It need not be an even thickness.

5. Bake for 2 hours. Probe the meringue with a small knife. If the center seems only slightly sticky, it will get crisp as it cools. When in doubt, bake a little longer. Turn off the oven and leave the meringue inside to cool.

6. When completely cool, break into one- to two-inch chunks and store in an airtight container. The meringue can be made up to 1 week ahead.

To assemble the dessert (begin at least 4 hours before serving but no more, as the whipped cream filling should not freeze completely):

1. Spread the ice cream evenly over the entire inside of a 4-quart metal bowl, cover with aluminum foil, and place in the freezer.

2. One to two hours before you are to eat the dessert, make the whipped cream and fold the chopped nougat into the larger portion.

3. Fill the ice-cream-lined mold with the whipped cream–nougat mixture.

4. Place the mold back in the freezer, covered with foil.

5. Remove from the freezer at least 15 minutes before serving. Let the mold sit for a few minutes, then unmold it onto a platter. If it does not come out, dip the mold into hot water for 15 seconds and try again.

6. Spread with the reserved whipped cream and cover with the chunks of meringue.

7. Sprinkle with the chocolate shavings.

8. Make sure the ice cream has softened a bit, then cut into wedges and serve. This dessert is spectacular look- ing, so be sure to serve at the table.

Bombe Pavillon

In his 1962 book *Dining at the Pavillon*, Joseph Wechsberg recalls a meal at the acclaimed French restaurant in New York City, at which he ordered the "'gourmet' dinner, the most refined, most delicate evening program in the restaurant's gastronomic repertory." The meal began with consommé royale, a subtle and intricate broth garnished with a tiny dice of rich egg custard. Then there was sole de la manche au vermouth, made with fish that had arrived from France just a few hours before; poularde demi-deuil, served with a 1937 Cheval Blanc, followed by Coeur de Laitue. Dessert was a Bombe Pavillon, which Wechsberg described on the second to last page as a "a delicious dessert—an elegant coffee-ice cream-inside-vanilla-ice cream ornament, topped by a mixture of pineapple, apples, peaches, and pears cooked in syrup, sprinkled with chopped nuts and with heated kirsch, and lighted." In *The Happy Years, Diaries 1944–1948*, Cecil Beaton describes lunching with Greta Garbo at Le Pavillon and also mentions loving this ice cream dessert, which he described as ice cream with hot prunes, pineapple, and nuts.

The Pavillon was opened by French chef Henri Soulé as an offshoot of his highly popular "Le Restaurant Pavillon de France," part of the 1939 New York World's Fair. The Pavillon was considered the top restaurant in the United States virtually until it closed in 1971. Soulé was called "the greatest living restaurateur" by the American epicure Lucius Beebe. And American culinary icon James Beard said "Henri Soulé is to be ranked with the greatest restaurateurs of Paris."

While I was attending cooking school at Peter Kump's (today the Institute of Culinary Education), Daniel Boulud was one of several guest chefs. He made a marvelous meal: potato galette with chicken livers and a ricotta-herb mix; cured duck pot au feu with an herb vinaigrette, and for dessert he prepared a fall fruit fricassee served over caramel ice cream. Reading about Soulé's bombe made me think back to that afternoon with Boulud and wonder if he too had read Wechsberg's book. Because I did not have Soulé's exact recipe, I used Boulud's fruit fricassee as a starting point and my imagination for the rest. Make the dessert with store-bought coffee ice cream or my adaptation of Chef Boulud's Caramel Ice Cream.

Serves 6 to 8

1 pint vanilla ice cream, best-quality store-bought or
    homemade (see recipe, page 190)
4 to 5 cups Caramel Ice Cream (recipe follows) or best-
    quality store-bought coffee ice cream
⅓ cup chopped toasted blanched almonds
Warm Fruit Compote (recipe follows)

To assemble:

1. Let the vanilla ice cream soften. Working quickly,
spoon it into a rinsed and damp 6-cup mold and use a
rubber spatula to line the sides and bottom of the mold
evenly with the ice cream.

2. Place the mold in the freezer for at least 30 minutes
to allow the ice cream to harden.

3. Let the caramel or coffee ice cream soften. Remove the
mold from the freezer and fill it with the caramel or coffee
ice cream. Smooth the top, cover tightly with foil, and
return to the freezer for at least 2 hours.

4. To serve, dip the mold in a bowl of hot water for 15
seconds and unmold the bombe onto a chilled serving
plate. Let the bombe soften a bit and sprinkle with
chopped almonds. Slice and serve with the Warm Fruit
Compote spooned over.

WARM FRUIT COMPOTE

½ small fresh pineapple (cut the pineapple vertically)
2 Golden Delicious apples, peeled, cored, and cut into
    wedges ½ inch thick
2 Anjou pears, peeled, cored, and cut into wedges
    ½ inch thick
Finely grated zest and juice of 1 lemon
Finely grated zest and juice of 1 orange
6 tablespoons unsalted butter
Small pinch of salt
3 tablespoons firmly packed brown sugar
1 vanilla bean, split and scraped
2 nectarines, halved, pitted, and cut into thin wedges
¼ cup raisins
2 dried figs, thinly sliced
8 pitted prunes, soaked in 3 tablespoons Calvados
    or other brandy for at least 6 hours
3 tablespoons Calvados or whatever brandy was
    previously used

1. Cut the half pineapple in half vertically. Use a small
knife to remove the rind, being sure to cut deep enough
to remove the "eyes." Slice crosswise into ¼-inch slices.

2. Toss the pineapple, apple, and pear slices with the
lemon zest and juice and orange zest. Set aside.

3. In a large skillet over high heat, melt the butter. Add the
fruit mixture and cook, tossing for 2 minutes. Add the salt,
brown sugar, vanilla bean and its seeds, nectarines, raisins,
and figs, and continue to toss over the heat for another
2 minutes. Add the prunes and their soaking liquid and
toss for 3 minutes more.

4. Warm the 3 tablespoons brandy in a small saucepan.
Remove the fruit from the heat. Pour in the warmed brandy
and carefully ignite it with a match. Stir until the flames die
out. Be careful not to catch anything on fire. Add the
orange juice and simmer for 1 minute more. The compote
can be prepared up to 2 hours in advance. Gently reheat
when ready to serve and pour into a deep bowl.

CARAMEL ICE CREAM

Makes approximately 3 pints

1 cup sugar
Small pinch of salt
1 vanilla bean, split and scraped
2 cups heavy cream
2 cups milk
6 large egg yolks

1. In a medium-sized saucepan, combine the sugar, salt,
vanilla bean with its seeds, and 2 tablespoons water. Stir
until the sugar dissolves, then cook over medium heat until
the sugar is deep brown, about 10 minutes; don't let it burn.

2. Carefully pour half of the cream and all the milk over
the caramel and stir until dissolved. This may need to be
done over the heat.

3. Whisk 2 tablespoons of the remaining cream together
with the egg yolks and add the mixture to the saucepan.
Cook over medium heat, stirring constantly, until thickened and almost simmering. Do not boil. Stir in the
remaining cream then pass the mixture through a sieve
into a bowl and let cool. Chill in the refrigerator until cold,
then freeze in an ice-cream maker according to manufacturer's instructions.

Bananas Foster

My ex-husband Willy wasn't much of a cook, but he did make one great dish that never failed to bring down the house. His Bananas Foster turned the refined dessert of his New Orleans childhood into something much more flavorful and robust. His secrets were to caramelize the sugar and bananas until almost burnt and to replace the white rum typically used in the original recipe with lots of Jamaican dark rum. In addition, he eliminated the banana liqueur as an unnecessary, prissy, and distracting frill. If you are curious, however, try adding a few tablespoons of banana liqueur along with the bananas.

After caramelizing an extravagance of brown sugar and butter with a touch of cinnamon and then bananas, Willy would set the whole mess (as that is certainly what it looked like by then) aflame with what seemed like an entire bottle of Myers's rum. Served over vanilla ice cream, these bananas are amazing. You will want to make extra, as everyone has seconds.

As the New Orleans Willy knew back then is gone, I feel his version of the recipe qualifies as lost. It is definitely well worth finding.

Serves 8

1 cup (2 sticks) unsalted butter
8 bananas, peeled and sliced in half lengthwise,
    then each piece cut in half crosswise
1¾ cups dark brown sugar
1 teaspoon ground cinnamon
Pinch of salt
1 cup dark rum
2 pints (1 quart) best-quality store-bought vanilla ice
    cream or homemade (see recipe, page 190)
8 pecan tuile cups (optional; see recipe for Almond Tuile
    Cups, page 27, and replace the almonds with
    chopped pecans)

1. In a large skillet over medium heat, melt the butter, then add the bananas in one layer.

2. Sprinkle with the brown sugar, cinnamon, and salt, and cook over medium heat, using a spatula to gently turn the bananas every couple of minutes, until the sugar melts and the sauce thickens and caramelizes. Don't let the sauce burn, but, short of burning, the more sticky and caramelized, the better.

3. Turn off the heat but leave the skillet on the burner. Stir in ¼ cup of the rum, being careful not to break up the bananas.

4. Meanwhile, warm the remaining rum in a small saucepan over medium heat. Pour the warmed rum into the bananas and carefully ignite with a match. Shake the pan and stir until all the flames die out. Be careful not to catch anything on fire.

5. Serve in dessert bowls over or under ice cream, or on dessert plates if you serve the bananas and ice cream in the tuiles.

Note: Willy did not use the tuile cups but they do serve to contain and beautify a somewhat messy dessert, making it more elegant. The tuiles are crispy and delicious, and the pecans make them very New Orleans. You can top the dessert with toasted pecans if you like.

ROMANOFF'S

Baked Alaska

Romanoff's restaurant was founded by one of the world's great imposters. Harry F. Gerguson was a flamboyant and highly successful restaurateur who passed himself off as Prince, or sometimes Duke, Michael Romanoff, although he spoke no Russian, was not related to any actual Russian aristocracy, and the real Prince Michael was killed in 1918 during the Russian Revolution. At other times Gerguson claimed to be a descendant of British prime minister William Gladstone and at others to have killed Rasputin. Despite (or because of) all these inventions, he charmed his way into Tinseltown society where his wit and incredible chutzpah were much appreciated.

He arrived in Hollywood from somewhere—some say he was born in Cincinnati, others say Brooklyn, and still others say Lithuania—in 1937 or 1938. A short, debonair "gentleman" with an Oxford accent, old-world manners, a Malacca walking stick, a monocle, spats, and a checkered past, he finagled his way into the movies, making brief appearances in *Fools for Scandal*, *Dancing in the Dark*, and *Sing While You're Able*, among others. Romanoff parlayed these silver-screen encounters into Hollywood friendships, and in 1939, Cary Grant, Darryl Zanuck, Jack Warner, Jock Whitney, and Robert Benchley loaned him $7,500 to start a restaurant. They expected failure and tax write-offs. Instead, Romanoff's opened in 1941 to huge crowds and rave reviews. It was an instant success, and within a year Prince Mike had bought out all his investors.

Gerguson may have been a phony, but he was a beloved phony with perfect taste. Because he served the best French food in Los Angeles, local gourmets and celebrities (Humphrey Bogart and Darryl Zanuck had their own booths; Clark Gable, Gary Cooper, Frank Sinatra, Groucho Marx, Jack Benny, and Cole Porter were regulars) tolerated his odd habits, which included frequently berating his best customers; sharing his dinner table with his two pet bulldogs, Socrates and Mr. Confucius; a close friendship with J. Edgar Hoover at a time when Hoover was reviled in Hollywood; and passing out unwanted right-wing literature along with the menus.

The raison d'etre of Baked Alaska is the contrast between the cold, smooth ice cream on the inside and the hot, chewy meringue on the outside. This novel dessert is achieved by insulating the ice cream with sponge cake beneath and meringue everywhere else, and then quickly browning the meringue in a hot oven and serving it immediately—with or without flames.

There is much controversy over the origins of this dessert, which in various forms was known in the nineteenth century as *omelette surprise*, *omelette à la norvegienne*, *glace au four* and, finally, as Baked Alaska. In early versions, fresh or candied fruit routinely appeared between the ice cream and the meringue, and the cake was often given a liqueur soak. The most elaborate version, *omelette en surprise Montmorency*, is surrounded by a flaming cherries jubilee. Montmorency is a village near Paris known for some of the finest cherries in France, hence the dessert's name.

In 1802 President Jefferson served a meal ending with ice cream wrapped in an insulating pastry crust before baking. Some say the first dessert of this kind incorporating meringue instead of pastry was invented in 1804 by an American statesman and physicist, Benjamin Rumford, who at the time was investigating the resistance of stiffly beaten egg whites to the induction of heat.

What we do know for sure is that in 1867 Charles Ranhofer, the French chef at the legendary Delmonico's restaurant in New York City—and famous for inventing lobster Newberg, chicken à la king, eggs Benedict, and Delmonico potatoes—used vanilla and banana ice creams along with apricot marmalade to create the Alaska-Florida Cake. It was made to celebrate the United States' purchase of Alaska from Russia. "Alaska-Florida" was soon changed to "Baked Alaska." The name stuck, and the dessert showed up on fancy restaurant menus in America well into the 1960s. The recipe provided is from the Rodeo Drive Romanoff's, which closed in 1962.

The first Baked Alaska I remember tasting was my mother's. She made it only for her grandest dinner parties and always with lemon custard ice cream. (On less grand occasions she baked lemon chiffon pie.) These two lemon and meringue creations prevailed at her dinners, except on the rare occasion when she was too busy for dessert-making and purchased a mocha buttercream genoise from Bailey's on Beverly Drive—our very-fabulous-for-the-1950s local French bakery—

or when, in cold weather (unusual in southern California), she concocted a trifle pudding by following Mr. Bailey's careful instructions.

I was little when first introduced to Baked Alaska—and my delight in the dessert was all the greater for having been allowed to enter the normally off-limits arena of "the adult dinner party." Before taking my first scrumptious, cold-lemon-ice-cream-plus-warm-meringue bite, there was the even greater excitement of seeing the flaming mountain of caramel-peaked whiteness brought to the table. My mother would snuggle a brandy-filled half eggshell into the top of the dessert, ignite the alcohol, and pray that nothing else caught on fire en route from kitchen to table. (In her divine book from 1922, *Kitchen Essays*, Lady Agnes Jekyll describes a visit to the Cannes Casino and viewing and then eating a similar flaming creation going by the name bombe Nero.)

Serves 10 to 12

For the cake:

⅓ cup sifted cake flour

½ teaspoon baking powder

⅛ teaspoon salt

2 large eggs, separated; reserve 1 yolk and both whites,
    at room temperature

⅓ cup granulated sugar

½ teaspoon grated orange zest

4 teaspoons boiling water

2 teaspoons fresh orange juice

½ teaspoon vanilla extract

½ teaspoon cream of tartar

For the meringue:

8 large egg whites, at room temperature

⅛ teaspoon salt

½ teaspoon cream of tartar

2 cups superfine sugar

2 teaspoons vanilla extract

For assembling:

2 to 3 tablespoons Grand Marnier, Cointreau,
    or Triple Sec (optional)

2 tablespoons granulated sugar

3 pints best-quality store-bought vanilla ice cream or
    homemade (see recipe, page 190), softened and
    shaped with your hands into an oval about 1-inch
    smaller all around than the size of your cake pan,
    wrapped in plastic and then foil, and frozen until very
    hard, at least 4 hours.

To make the cake:

1. Preheat the oven to 350 degrees. Butter and flour the bottom of an oval pan approximately 12 by 8 inches. (You can use a ceramic gratin dish if you don't have an oval metal cake pan; a 10-inch round cake pan may also be substituted.) Line the bottom with parchment paper; butter the paper.

2. Sift the flour together with the baking powder and salt, and set aside.

3. Beat the egg yolk until very light, several minutes.

4. Add the sugar and the orange zest to the egg yolk and beat until well combined. Add the boiling water and beat for 1 minute. Beat in the orange juice and vanilla.

5. Add the dry ingredients and beat until just combined.

6. Using an electric mixer fitted with the whisk attachment, whisk the two egg whites on low speed until foamy. Add the cream of tartar and beat on medium. When the egg whites are opaque, increase the speed to high and beat until stiff but not dry.

7. Stir one quarter of the beaten egg whites into the batter. Pour the lightened batter over the egg whites and fold until just combined.

8. Scrape the batter into the prepared pan. Smooth the top with a spatula and bake in the center of the oven until a cake tester inserted in the center comes out clean and the cake springs back when gently pressed, 15 to 20 minutes. Cool upside down on a wire rack. When completely cool, loosen the sides of the cake with a small knife, turn the cake onto your hand, and then invert it back onto the rack or an ovenproof serving platter if using immediately. Wrapped well, the cake may be made ahead and refrigerated for up to 2 days or frozen for up to 4 weeks.

To make the meringue:
1. Using an electric mixer fitted with the whisk attachment, beat the egg whites and salt on low speed until foamy. Add the cream of tartar and beat on medium speed until soft peaks form. Beating constantly, add the superfine sugar in a slow, steady stream. Add the vanilla and beat on high speed until the egg whites are very stiff. Set aside for no longer than 10 minutes, just while you prepare the ice cream.

To assemble the dessert:
1. Preheat the oven to 500 degrees (if your oven doesn't go that high, as close to 500 as possible).
2. Place the cake (it can be used straight out of the freezer) on an ovenproof oval platter. Drizzle with the liqueur, if using.
3. Unwrap the ice cream oval and place it on top of the cake, making sure the cake border is even all around the ice cream. Using a spatula, decoratively swirl all the meringue over the cake and ice cream, running the meringue down to the platter; work quickly as the ice

cream must remain very cold and hard. Make sure the cake and ice cream are completely sealed in by the meringue. (If you want, you can put some of the meringue in a pastry bag at this point and pipe decorations on top.) Sprinkle the 2 tablespoons sugar over the meringue and immediately place the platter in the upper third of the oven. Cook until lightly browned, 3 to 5 minutes, watching carefully. Serve immediately, before the ice cream melts. (If you wish, after the dessert is removed from the oven, spoon 2 additional tablespoons of liqueur on the platter around the dessert or in an eggshell you've half nestled into the meringue before baking. Ignite the liqueur with a long kitchen match. But be very careful, as the meringue can catch on fire.)

Notes: I like this dessert with a different flavored ice cream, such as lemon curd or coffee; if you're using vanilla ice cream, try serving with strawberry or Raspberry Sauce (see recipe, page 190).

This recipe uses raw egg whites. If you are concerned about bacteria, or if serving to the young, elderly, or those with health issues, use pasteurized egg whites or liquid egg whites as a substitute. Also, there's less risk of bacteria with organic eggs.

Peach Melba

When London's Carlton Hotel, the fifth in a succession of brilliant, acclaimed collaborations between Auguste Escoffier and César Ritz, opened on July 1, 1899, Peach Melba was on the opening-night menu. Escoffier had befriended Dame Nellie Melba, the famous Australian opera diva, in the mid-1890s when he ran the kitchen at the Savoy. She lived at the hotel on several different occasions while performing at Covent Garden. Dame Nellie loved luxury and good food, and became a serious fan of the great chef and restaurateur. Escoffier went on to create several other dishes for her including *poires* and *fraises Melba*, but they never gained the fame of her *peche* namesake.

In 1890 Dame Nellie was romantically involved with the fourteenth duke of Orleans, son and heir to the comte de Paris, the Bourbon pretender to the throne of Republican France. Tall, handsome, highly educated, and a delightful companion, he and Dame Nellie fell madly in love, and he accompanied her as she sang her way around the world. Dame Nellie had a husband (he was suing her for divorce and citing the duke) and the duke was not allowed to marry a commoner (or a Protestant or a married person, for that matter) so their affair was doomed from the start. However, during the several years it lasted, it was the royal love scandal of the decade and provided endless fodder for the tabloids.

By 1894 things between Dame Nellie and the duke were rocky. In an attempt to patch things up, she asked Escoffier to help her organize an intimate dinner with her lover and a few friends to take place at the Savoy after one of her *Lohengrin* performances. Marie Louise Ritz, widow of César, writes in her book *César Ritz, Host to the World*, that Peach Melba, "one of Escoffier's happiest inventions," was a serendipitous compromise between Dame Melba, who wanted to end the meal with peches flambées, a hot dessert, and the chef, who insisted that ice cream would be better.

Escoffier's story in *Memories of My Life* differs slightly. He says he had "wanted to create a surprise for her" and "seized the occasion." To commemorate the "majestic and mythical" swan that appears in the first act of the opera, Escoffier sculpted a swan out of a large block of ice. He placed vanilla ice cream, fresh peaches, and sweetened fresh raspberry purée in a silver bowl, nestled this creation between the wings of the ice bird, and spun a lacy web of sugar over the top. Melba "was delighted," and if Escoffier did say so himself, "the effect was stunning." A number of years later, when her love life went completely awry, she became despondent and put on weight. Escoffier was again called to the rescue, and invented Melba toast.

Emperor Wilhelm II once told Auguste Escoffier, "I am the emperor of Germany, but you are the emperor of chefs." King of chefs and chef of kings, Escoffier is considered by many (Carême being the only real contender) to be the greatest chef of all time. He is responsible for thousands of recipes. His peach desserts alone—and this is in no way a complete list—include *Alexandra*, *Cardinal*, *au Chateau-Lafite*, *dame blanche*, *petit-duc*, *rose-cheri*, *Trianon*, *bohemienne*, and the especially delicious, *peches Eugenie*, incorporating wild strawberries, Kirsch, maraschino, and Champagne zabaglione; but Peach Melba is, by far, the most famous.

In the 1920s, almost thirty years after the dessert was first served, Escoffier was irritated by the fact that, though made frequently, it was rarely made properly. He wrote, "Peach melba is a simple dish made up of tender and very ripe peaches, vanilla ice cream, and a purée of sugared raspberry. Any variation of this recipe ruins the delicate balance of its taste." He goes on to mention specific misuse of jams and jellies, whipped cream, and even arrowroot and other floury substances to thicken the berries. An extreme example of the liberties taken with Peach Melba appears in the otherwise quite delightful *Alice B. Toklas Cookbook*, in which the eccentric Toklas gives her verison of the dessert, omitting the ice cream, one of only three basic ingredients.

Misinformation is rampant, so here is the recipe exactly as written in *Auguste Escoffier, Memories of My Life*, with my addition of American measurements in parentheses. If, by chance, you are not in possession of a silver timbale, or are too busy to carve an ice sculpture or make spun sugar, just place the ice cream in a glass bowl or other attractive serving dish, arrange the peaches on top, and pour the raspberry sauce over. The spirit of Escoffier will not be lost. Use high-quality store-bought vanilla ice cream or make your own (see recipe, page 190). If you want to experiment with the spun sugar, see recipe, page 191.

Serves 6

Choose 6 tender and perfectly ripe peaches. The Montreuil peach, for example, is perfect for this dessert. Blanch the peaches for 2 seconds in boiling water, remove them immediately with a slotted spoon, and place them in iced water for a few seconds. Peel them and place them on a plate, sprinkle them with a little sugar, and refrigerate them. Prepare a liter [1 quart] of very creamy vanilla ice cream and a purée of 250 grams [2½ cups] of very ripe raspberries crushed through a fine sieve and mixed with 150 grams [½ cup] of powdered sugar. Refrigerate.

To serve: Fill a silver timbale with the vanilla ice cream. Delicately place the peaches on top of the ice cream and cover with the raspberry purée. Optionally, during the almond season, one can add a few slivers of fresh almonds on top, but never use dried almonds.

Presentation: Embed the silver timbale in an ice sculpture and add a lace of spun sugar over the peaches.

ANTONIN CARÊME'S

Nectarine Plombière

In an era when "it was permissible to steal lovers or mistresses, but an unforgivable crime to purloin a rival's chef," according to George Lang's *Compendium of Culinary Nonsense and Trivia*, an invitation to a Carême banquet, a three-star destination, was prized by the crowned, titled, and elite the world over. Many consider Antonin Carême to be the greatest chef of all time. He was self-educated, but as Anne Willan noted in *Great Cooks and Their Recipes*, his intellect allowed him "to analyze cooking old and new, to simplify methods and menus, and to define every aspect of the art that today is known as *haute cuisine*. He also had a practical brilliance that led him to become the most sought-after chef of his generation. . . . Like Napoleon he combined, on his own level, a classic sense of order with romantic ambitions and a flair for self-dramatization."

This culinary genius conceived the Soufflé Rothschild (page 164) in the early 1820s. During an intense and spectacular career, he invented ladyfingers, vol-au-vents, Nesselrode pudding, riz à l'imperatrice, the large meringue, gateau pithiviers, the bouquet garni, and the pastry bag, along with hundreds of soup and sauce recipes, the latter including the three classics—espagnole, béchamel, and velouté.

Born in 1783 into abject poverty, Carême was the sixteenth of twenty-four siblings. In 1792, when he was nine and Paris was in the midst of revolution, Antonin's father left him in the street to fend for himself, supposedly with the words "fare well in the world . . . for those like you, with quick wits, there are great fortunes to be made." Luckily, for the history of "la cuisine" he was rescued almost immediately by the owner of a local chophouse. After a few years, Carême left her to apprentice at Bailly's, a fashionable patisserie on rue Vivienne. The kind and generous Monsieur Bailly encouraged the illiterate Carême to spend afternoons in the print room of the National Library, where he taught himself to both draw and read. These hours of study provided the foundation for his future elaborate pastry creations. Carême became at least as famous for his architectural confectionary centerpieces as for his recipes and was eventually nicknamed "Le Palladio de la patisserie."

Before long, Charles-Maurice de Talleyrand heard of Carême's spectacular success, bustled into Bailly's, and swept the young chef off to manage his own pastry kitchen. The foreign minister under Napoleon and later Louis XVIII, Talleyrand was known for maintaining one of the best tables in all of France. It was in his kitchen, working alongside Talleyrand's head chef, Boucher, that Carême learned the job of "chef de cuisine," emulating and eventually surpassing his teacher. Carême's culinary brilliance allowed the foreign minister to use gastronomy as an effective diplomatic tool. Carême's career as a culinary diplomat continued while working for the prince regent of England, Tsar Alexander I of Russia, and both the Viennese and British courts. Even Napoleon and Josephine's wedding cake was a Carême creation. Carême did all of this and more before 1823, when at age thirty-one he went to work for Jacob and Betty de Rothschild, and his gastronomic golden days began in earnest.

An immigrant German Jew, Jacob (called James in France) de Rothschild had wealth to dwarf that of most European monarchs. However, he was unknown in France's aristocratic and somewhat anti-Semitic circles until he married his sophisticated young cousin Betty. The pair launched a successful campaign to win over French society by hiring Carême and exploiting his culinary artistry. Lunches for thirty were followed by dinners for sixty virtually every day of the week in a ballroom that could accommodate three thousand guests with a stage large enough to hold a forty-piece orchestra.

For many years, a Carême meal chez Rothschild was the hottest ticket in Paris, if not all of Europe. The guests frequently included the Continent's artistic and intellectual elite—Hugo, Balzac, Ingres, Chopin, Liszt, and Rossini—as well as aristocrats and politicians. Carême was in the press constantly. With his name linked to the great artists and musicians of the age, he became the world's first—and for a long time only—celebrity chef. Newfound financial security enabled him to fulfill his lifelong dream of writing a lasting contribution to food literature, the masterpiece *L'art de la cuisine francaise au 19ième siecle*, an encyclopedia of thousands of recipes and the complete "how to" of "haute cusine." Unfortunately, years of hard and ceaseless work took its toll on his health. Carême died in 1833 at the age of fifty, "burnt out by the flame of his genius and the charcoal of the roasting-spit" (Laurent Tailhade) but not before declaring, "Charcoal kills us, but what does it matter? The shorter the life, the greater the glory."

In his 1847 novel *Splendeurs et misères des courtisanes*, Honoré de Balzac writes, "After supper, ices by the name of plombières were served. Everyone knows that this type of ice is arranged in a pyramid with a small, very delicate crystallized fruit placed on the surface." *Larousse Gastronomique* describes the plombière as "an ice cream made with custard cream . . . usually enriched with whipped cream and mixed with crystallized fruit steeped in kirsch," and states that it gets its name from the lead (*plomb*) mold in which it was traditionally made.

Carême created his Nectarine Plombière on July 6, 1829, in honor of famous food and travel writer, Irish radical and wit, Lady Morgan, who was dining chez Rothschild that evening. Carême used nectarines picked from the gardens at dawn to create a mountain of lightly frozen ambrosial

nectarine cream. Along with orange jelly–stuffed oranges, the plombière ended an elaborate "service à la francaise" dinner that included two soups, cod with hollandaise, sea bass "à l'italienne," leg of lamb, a chartreuse of quail, vol-au-vents, filet of beef, glazed rabbit with chicory, roast chicken, bacon-larded pigeon, and several vegetables. The table was reset twice with plates and cutlery, but *la sultane à la colonne*, a huge and spectacular spun-sugar extravaganza in the form of a classical Greek temple, remained as the centerpiece from start to finish, specifically to flatter the guest of honor: on the temple column closest to her, "Lady Morgan" was written in royal icing. Carême and the Rothschilds wanted her ladyship to applaud the evening in writing, and in her new book, *France in 1829–30*, she certainly did:

> *and the tempered chill of the plombière . . . anticipated the strongest shock, and broke it, of the exquisite avalanche, which, with the hue and odour of fresh gathered nectarines, [which] satisfied every sense and dissipated every coarser flavour . . . If crowns were distributed to cooks as to actors . . . [one] should have graced the brow of Carême for this specimen of the intellectual perfection of an art, the standard and gauge of modern civilization!*

Serves 12 generously

15 very ripe or even overripe nectarines, plus 3 barely ripe nectarines, sliced into very thin wedges, for garnish

½ cup sugar

Large pinch of salt

4 large egg yolks

1 tablespoon rice flour, cornstarch, or all-purpose flour

2½ cups milk

4 cups of very cold heavy cream

1 teaspoon vanilla extract

3 tablespoons peach-flavored or maraschino liqueur (optional)

Raspberries, blackberries, currants, and/or fraises de bois (optional)

1. Peel and pit the 15 ripe nectarines. Cut them into chunks and place them in a 2-quart saucepan with 6 tablespoons of the sugar and the salt. Cook over medium heat, stirring frequently, until thick and syrupy, 10 to 20 minutes depending on the ripeness of the fruit. Test the mixture by cooling a teaspoonful on a plate. It should have the consistency of jam. If it is too thin, cook and test until the proper consistency.

2. Press the nectarine "jam" through a sieve into a large bowl and let cool.

3. Place the egg yolks, rice flour (or cornstarch or all-purpose flour) and milk in a 1-quart saucepan. Whisk to combine. Over low heat, stir constantly until the mixture begins to thicken. Simmer, continuing to stir, for 3 minutes; the mixture should thicken considerably. Off of the heat, add the remaining 2 tablespoons sugar and stir until dissolved.

4. Pour the egg mixture into the bowl with the cooled fruit purée. Place in a larger bowl of ice water until cool. Stir occasionally. When cool, cover and refrigerate for up to 2 days.

5. Two to four hours before serving, whip the cream together with the vanilla; fold the whipped cream into the very cold fruit mixture. Spoon this plombière mixture into a bowl or large decorative mold (3 to 4 quarts). Place in the freezer for 2 to 4 hours, folding gently with a rubber spatula every 30 minutes or so. The plombière should be gently set but not frozen rock hard. If frozen a day or two in advance, be sure to let the dessert sit at room temperature until softened, 15 to 30 minutes before serving.

6. Serve in glass bowls garnished with the nectarine slices and berries if using. If you used a mold, unmold (dip the mold into hot water for 15 seconds if necessary) and garnish with the sliced nectarines and berries.

C. C. BROWN'S

Hot Fudge Sundae

A favorite treat of my very ice creamy childhood was a hot fudge sundae at C. C. Brown's on Hollywood Boulevard. I would sit at the counter or on a pink leather banquette in one of the dark mahogany booths and order my sundae. A scoop of vanilla ice cream topped with whipped cream and toasted almonds would arrive in a "silver goblet." The "secret recipe" hot fudge sauce was always served in a little brown ceramic pitcher alongside.

In 1906, the same decade that Hershey's made its first milk chocolate bar, local Hollywood lore has it that Clarence Clifton Brown invented the hot fudge sundae. In 1929 C. C. Brown's moved from downtown Los Angeles to the corner of Hollywood and Vine, where the restaurant existed in its original form until it closed for good in 1996.

During the film industry's golden age, this soda fountain was a frequent hangout of big-studio celebrities and wannabes. Joan Crawford, Walt Disney, and Bob Hope were regulars as was Marlon Brando, who was "discovered" there while working as a waiter.

After a premiere down the block at Grauman's Chinese Theater, fans lined up outside of Brown's waiting for hours to get autographs from the movie stars inside. I did not care about the autographs; the only draw for me was warm chocolate becoming sticky and delicious as it hardened on cold ice cream. In combination with the darkly roasted almonds, this sundae was the best thing I had ever tasted. I've summoned up taste memories from that distant past to re-create this delicious sauce.

Serves 1

2 scoops best-quality store-bought vanilla ice cream
    or homemade (see recipe, page 190)
Lightly sweetened whipped cream (optional)
About 3 tablespoons very coarsely chopped toasted
    blanched almonds
About ¼ cup warm C. C. Brown's Hot Fudge Sauce
    (recipe follows)

1. Place the ice cream in a cold (preferably metal) ice-cream cup or a bowl.
2. Top with a dollop of whipped cream, if desired, and sprinkle the nuts on top. To replicate the presentation at C. C. Brown's, serve a small pitcher of the hot fudge sauce with each portion. Or top each ice cream portion with the sauce, then the whipped cream, followed by the nuts.

Makes about 2½ cups, enough for about
10 sundaes

2 tablespoons unsweetened cocoa powder
2 cups sugar
1½ cups heavy cream
½ cup light corn syrup
½ cup unsweetened chocolate, chopped
2 teaspoons vanilla extract
⅛ teaspoon of salt
¼ teaspoon malt or cider vinegar

1. In a large heavy saucepan, stir together the cocoa, sugar, and ½ cup of the cream until smooth.
2. Stir in the rest of the cream, followed by the corn syrup, and chopped chocolate. Insert a candy thermometer. Bring to a boil over medium heat and cook without stirring until it reaches 236 degrees.
3. Off the heat, stir in the vanilla extract, salt, and vinegar. Serve the sauce lukewarm.

Note: Store the sauce in the refrigerator in a covered jar. To reheat, remove the lid and microwave briefly or heat the jar in a saucepan filled with enough boiling water to come halfway up its sides.

ANTONIN CARÊME'S

Strawberries Romanoff

Strawberry desserts are variations on a theme. There are hundreds if not thousands of them in the French repertoire alone. One of the simplest and most delicious is Antonin Carême's Strawberries Romanoff, nothing but perfectly ripe strawberries macerated in curaçao and orange juice, then topped with whipped cream. The late Mike Romanoff (of the now-defunct Romanoff's in Beverly Hills) claimed to have invented the dessert; however, food historians are fairly certain it was created by Carême around 1815. At that time, he was cooking for Tsar Alexander I, a Romanoff, who was living in the Élysées Palace after having "liberated" Paris from Napoleon.

The flavor combination of orange and strawberry is the defining characteristic of Carême's dessert. French distilleries of the day were experimenting with Triple Sec curaçao (a brandy produced since the 1500s on the Caribbean island of the same name that incorporated the peel of bitter oranges). Because of the popularity of this orange liqueur, Carême used it extensively. He created both French and Russian versions of this dessert, the only difference being that the Russian variant had sour cream mixed with the whipped cream. Later the Americans came up with their own adaptation, garnishing the berries with vanilla ice cream.

In his *Compendium of Culinary Nonsense and Trivia*, George Lang claims that the original Strawberries Romanoff is something else entirely: crushed strawberries soaked overnight in good red port, then puréed and sieved over more strawberries arranged in a crystal serving dish or in individual glass bowls. Authentic or not, Lang's recipe tastes too good not to mention.

Carême's French version is provided here.

Serves 4

4 cups small, perfectly ripe strawberries, washed and hulled
Juice of 1 orange
¼ cup curaçao
1 cup very cold heavy cream
¼ cup superfine sugar
½ teaspoon vanilla extract
½ cup sour cream (optional)
1 pint best-quality store-bought vanilla ice cream or homemade (see recipe, page 190), optional

1. Stir the strawberries together with the orange juice and curaçao and place, covered, in the refrigerator for at least 1 hour.
2. Whip the cream with the sugar and vanilla until soft peaks form. Fold in the sour cream, if using.
3. Place the strawberries in a bowl, on top of the ice cream if using, with a dollop of the cream. Do not mix together. Serve immediately.

THE ZODIAC ROOM'S

Toasted Pecan Balls

Once upon a time there was only one Neiman Marcus in the world, and it was the store to top all stores. Located in downtown Dallas, Neiman's was the ultimate destination for luxurious, self-indulgent, over-the-top shopping for the rich and the very rich. In addition to creating the first truly high-end Christmas catalogue, featuring such unique and fanciful items as "his and hers" hot-air balloons, Chinese junks, and Egyptian mummy cases, in 1953 Neiman Marcus did something revolutionary for the time: it put a restaurant—the Zodiac Room—in a department store. The stated rationale was "a sated shopper is a happy shopper." At first it was a disappointment: the food, service, buzz, and flair were not up to the very high Neiman Marcus standards. But when Stanley Marcus hired Helen Corbitt to run the restaurant and address its failings, everything changed.

Corbitt was a Yankee who moved south, first to Austin, then to Dallas. An authority on food, she became a minor celebrity and was admired far and wide for her culinary accomplishments. Marcus declared her "the Balenciaga of food," the Duke of Windsor once asked her how she made her avocado mousse; governors, politicians, college presidents, oilmen, and literary figures sang her praises.

She was known for her dramatic and unusual food presentation before such presentation became commonplace. One of Corbitt's signature desserts was a Baked Alaska that arrived in a terra-cotta flower pot with a real flower sticking out of the meringue topping. And children loved her ice-cream clowns with ice-cream-cone hats and candy faces.

Corbitt's impact was so great that many people in Dallas and beyond think of her with admiration and affection to this day. In addition to being the "first lady of the kitchen" at Neiman Marcus, she transformed retail dining in America by raising the culinary bar and inspiring others to follow her example. Stanley Marcus called her his "wild Irish genius" because of her uncontrollability, her quick temper, and her culinary brilliance.

Signature dishes included a complimentary demitasse of chicken broth served as an amuse-gueule; a basket of oven-fresh banana and monkey breads, cinnamon buns, and mini corn muffins; and her famous fruit salad with poppyseed dressing. Two memorable dessert recipes, Caramel Soufflé (page 174) and Toasted Pecan Balls, are shared here.

A Corbitt classic, Toasted Pecan Balls are easy to make and delicious, the sum much better than the simple parts: ice-cream balls rolled in toasted pecans and topped with hot fudge sauce. This dessert dates back to Corbitt's pre–Neiman Marcus days in the early 1950s, when she ran the dining room at the Driskill Hotel in Austin.

You can experiment with the nuts: toasted hazelnuts, walnuts, peanuts, or even pignoli are nice. Corbitt recommends a variation using toasted, slivered almonds; but her original pecans provide a special Texas flavor, a "spirit of place." Try topping the hot fudge sauce with two or three tablespoons of warm Butterscotch Sauce (see page 159). The sauces become chewy when they hit the cold ice cream, and, along with the pecans, combine in the bowl to create an ice cream-cum-"turtle" dessert. Paired with coffee ice cream, this combination is beyond divine. Whipped cream on the side is an extra indulgence—but why not?

Serves 6

1½ pints best-quality store-bought vanilla, chocolate, or coffee ice cream or homemade (see recipe, page 190)
3 cups toasted pecans, broken into small pieces
1½ cups C. C. Brown's Hot Fudge Sauce (see page 150)

1. At least 1 hour before serving, place six ½-cup scoops of ice cream on a baking sheet that will fit in your freezer. (Place the baking sheet in the freezer beforehand, so it is cold.)
2. Using your hands or large spoons, shape the ice cream into 6 smooth balls. Place in the freezer to harden.
3. Place the nuts in a cake pan with sides. Then, roll one ice cream ball at a time in the pecans, gently pressing the nuts into the ice cream so they adhere.
4. Store the balls in the freezer on the baking sheet until ready to serve. Cover with plastic wrap or aluminum foil if you will not be serving them within 1 hour.

5. To serve, let the balls soften at room temperature for 5 to 10 minutes; you do not want them to be rock hard. Spoon 2 tablespoons of warm hot fudge sauce into each of 6 dessert bowls. Top with the frozen ice cream balls and spoon 2 more tablespoons of the warm hot fudge sauce over the top of each portion. Serve immediately.

Notes: These sundaes are even better with the addition of 2 or 3 tablespoons per sundae of Schrafft's Butterscotch Sauce (see page 159). If the sauce is cold, reheat it until warm and melted, for 30 to 60 seconds in a microwave oven or in an open jar set in a pan of simmering water.

Corbitt's coconut balls are made the same way: Just roll chocolate or vanilla ice cream balls in grated, lightly toasted coconut (fresh, if possible). Corbitt suggests serving them with mashed raspberries or strawberries, or a lemon custard sauce. I prefer hot fudge sauce here, too.

Brown Bread Ice Cream

Brown Bread Ice Cream tastes infinitely better than the name suggests, getting its unique flavor from deeply caramelizing brown bread crumbs with sugar and butter before incorporating them into the cream.

Easy to make, rich, and delicious, this frozen delight does not require an ice-cream maker. Whipped cream is folded into a cooled custard along with the caramelized crumbs. The mixture is then put in the freezer to harden, more in the manner of the frozen mousses and bombes dating back to Carême than a true ice cream.

Fruit iced creams became popular in Britain in the eighteenth century in conjunction with the arrival of ice houses on country estates. Brown Bread Ice Cream, an early version of "cookies 'n' cream," soon followed but did not become popular until Queen Victoria's time, when it was regularly served as a country-weekend treat. In *Harvest of the Cold Months*, celebrated British food writer Elizabeth David describes her experiences in the summer of 1934, when the entire cast of *A Midsummer Night's Dream* (she was a fledgling actress and stage manager) was treated to "slightly crunchy, grainy, bisque-colored brown bread ice cream that came out of those pots in a seemingly endless supply of voluptuous scoops." Eric Boman remembers eating the ice cream in the 1970s; it was a staple dessert at Provan's, the London restaurant owned by his friend Stuart Grimshaw, who says that, like French toast and bread pudding, this ice cream was originally a way to use up old bread.

There are many versions of the recipe, some using only cream and no eggs, some omitting the liquor, some not toasting the crumbs (this omission misses the entire point of the dessert), and some toasting the bread crumbs but not caramelizing them (also a mistake). This recipe is an adaptation of my favorite: John Howard's version from Le Coq Hardi, Dublin's premier restaurant and an Irish institution for almost twenty-five-years until it closed its doors in 2001. Howard served the ice cream alongside ginger crème brûlée, but that gilds the lily. I find that the ice cream stands alone just fine—and alone is the best way to appreciate its elusive mingled tastes of caramel, rum, egg, and crunchy bread crumbs.

For the crumbs I've adapted a wonderful recipe for Irish Brown Bread that my Irish friend David Nolan, a Manhattan-based art dealer, spirited away from his mother. The bread is quick and easy to put together, as it gets its rise from baking soda instead of yeast. This grainy, rich-tasting bread makes the most healthful and marvelous breakfast toast I know; and buttered, it is the perfect complement for smoked salmon or gravlax. If you are not up to making your own bread, bakery whole wheat or seven-grain makes excellent caramelized crumbs, but I jump at any excuse to bake this unsurpassable Irish brown bread.

A shortcut used at the Ballymaloe—a paradise of a hotel and restaurant and the place just outside Cork where I tasted this ice cream for the first time—is to make the sugared crumbs and fold them and the (optional) liquor into three pints of softened vanilla ice cream, and then refreeze. Their ice cream is served with a black and red currant compote made by heating some sugar and twice its weight in currants with a pinch of salt in a saucepan set over medium heat. When the sugar has dissolved and the fruit is soft, remove from the heat and cool before serving.

Makes approximately 2 quarts

5 tablespoons unsalted butter
1¾ cups stale, dry, coarse brown bread crumbs, preferably made from Irish Brown Bread (recipe follows)
½ cup plus 2 tablespoons dark brown sugar
4 large eggs, separated, at room temperature
½ cup superfine sugar
½ teaspoon vanilla extract
1 tablespoon (or more to taste) of rum, brandy, or Madeira (optional)
1¾ cups very cold heavy cream
Pinch of salt

1. In a small skillet, melt the butter and then add the bread crumbs. Fry, stirring frequently, until the bread crumbs are beginning to crisp (5 to 10 minutes), then add the brown sugar. Cook the mixture, stirring occasionally, until the sugar melts and becomes dark and caramelized, 5 to 10 minutes. Remove from the heat, turn the contents of the pan out onto a piece of foil and let cool completely. Place the bread crumbs in a plastic bag and crush them with a rolling pin, or pulse them a few times in a food processor to grind coarsely.
2. Beat the egg yolks together with the superfine sugar, vanilla, and liqueur, if using, until pale and fluffy. Whip the cream until soft peaks form (do not overbeat). Fold the whipped cream into the egg yolk mixture.
3. Using an electric mixer fitted with the whisk attachment, beat the room temperature egg whites together with the salt until stiff but not dry; fold them into the whipped cream and egg mixture. Fold in the crushed bread crumbs.
4. Freeze in a lidded container (just large enough to hold the mixture with a little room for expansion) for at least 4 hours or until hard. This can be done a week or more in advance. Thaw 20 minutes before serving.

IRISH BROWN BREAD

Makes 2 (9-by-5-inch) loaves

3 cups stone-ground whole wheat flour
1⅓ cups self-rising flour
2 cups natural wheat bran
1½ cups steel-cut oats
4 teaspoons baking soda
2 tablespoons dark brown sugar
1½ teaspoons sea salt
½ cup wheat germ
1 quart plus ¾ cup buttermilk, at room temperature

1. Preheat the oven to 400 degrees. Grease two 9-by-5-inch loaf pans.
2. In a large bowl, use a large spoon to stir all the ingredients except the buttermilk together until well combined.
3. Add the buttermilk and stir until the dry ingredients are evenly moist.
4. Divide the dough equally between the prepared bread pans. Bake in the middle of the preheated oven for 50 minutes. Unmold and cool on wire racks.

Famous Butterscotch Sundae

My father, a transplanted New Yorker living in California, regaled us with the joys of Schrafft's as far back as I can remember. His descriptions were much like those of Jeremiah Tower in his *New American Classics* (1986): "I remember hot, humid days in Manhattan, walking along hoping I would pass a Schrafft's so that I could nip into the air-conditioned room, sit at the cool marble counter, and order a Black-and-White [ice cream soda]."

Back then, Schrafft's tearooms dotted the city; you could always find one nearby. I found many on my trips to New York and probably tasted every ice cream creation on the menu. Two absolute favorites were the Coffee Milkshake, intensely flavored with coffee syrup, and the famous Butterscotch Sundae, with a sauce that whispered of hot molasses and a whipped cream topping sprinkled with unexpectedly salty whole almonds.

Sadly, the last Schrafft's closed its doors in 1980. But on a hot day, I like to make one of Schrafft's superlative ice-cream treats, taste it, close my eyes, and travel back in time.

To authentically re-create this sundae, use store-bought whole salted almonds in their skins—not dry-roasted, not gourmet, but rather the old-fashioned ones commonly served with cocktails in the 1960s and 1970s. Although not quite authentic, sprinkling the sundae with roasted and salted Marcona almonds is a delicious update.

For one sundae

¼ cup warm Schrafft's Authentic Butterscotch Sauce (recipe follows)

2 scoops best-quality store-bought vanilla ice cream or homemade (see recipe, page 190)

Large dollop of whipped cream

About 6 whole salted almonds (skins on)

1. Put 1 tablespoon of the sauce in the bottom of a metal tulip cup or bowl. Scoop the ice cream on top. Pour the rest of the warm sauce over the ice cream, then sprinkle with the nuts and top with the whipped cream. Serve immediately.

SCHRAFFT'S AUTHENTIC BUTTERSCOTCH SAUCE

Makes approximately 3 cups,
enough for about 10 sundaes

1⅓ cups granulated sugar
1⅓ cups packed dark brown sugar
¼ teaspoon salt
1 cup light corn syrup
⅔ cup hot water
1⅔ cups heavy cream
2 teaspoons vanilla extract

1. Butter the bottom and sides of a heavy, medium-sized saucepan. Put the sugars and salt in the saucepan. Add the corn syrup and hot water. Bring the mixture to a boil over medium heat, stirring constantly.
2. As soon as the mixture boils, turn the heat up to medium-high and cover the saucepan tightly. Boil the mixture for 3 minutes. Uncover the saucepan and insert a candy thermometer. Stirring often, cook the syrup until it reaches 290 degrees. Remove from the heat and let cool for 3 to 4 minutes.
3. Stir 1 cup of the cream into the syrup. If the syrup mixture stiffens, don't worry. As you heat it with the cream, it will dissolve.
4. Return the saucepan to medium heat. Cook the syrup until it reaches 250 degrees.
5. Once again, remove from the heat and let the syrup cool for several minutes. Stir in the remaining ⅔ cup cream. Stirring constantly, bring the sauce to a rolling boil; remove from the heat as soon as it reaches a full boil. Let cool for 5 minutes, then stir in the vanilla. Stir the sauce occasionally as it cools. Serve the sauce lukewarm. Store it in the refrigerator in a covered jar, and reheat it until warm, for 30 to 60 seconds in a microwave oven or in an open jar set in a pan of simmering water.

SCHRAFFT'S
Coffee Milkshake

Serves 1

¼ cup Coffee Syrup (recipe follows)
2⅔ cups best-quality store-bought coffee ice cream, softened
1 cup half-and-half
1½ cups whole milk

1. Place all ingredients in a blender and process just until combined. Pour into a tall cold glass.

COFFEE SYRUP

Makes 1 cup

1 cup sugar
¼ cup instant espresso powder, such as Medaglio D'Oro
¼ teaspoon vanilla extract

1. Combine the sugar, instant espresso powder, and 1 cup water in a small saucepan. Simmer over low heat for 5 minutes. Remove from heat. When cool, stir in the vanilla. The syrup can be stored in the refrigerator for many months.

Flaming Tahitian Ice Cream

Victor Bergeron, known to the world as Trader Vic, is perhaps best known for inventing the Mai Tai. In Tahitian the words mean "out of this world, the best," which is how thousands of fans rated the food and drink at his restaurants. Vic was famous for both rum and flaming (many of his main courses, in addition to the drinks, arrived at the table still burning). The Flaming Tahitian Ice Cream is one of his best dessert creations, combining tropical fruit; a hot, rum-based sauce; and cold, creamy coconut ice cream.

Trader Vic was also a pioneer of fusion food. He served his own distinctive version of Polynesian dishes, and was ahead of his time in his use of fresh and exotic ingredients. With tropical drinks as strong as his vocabulary and one of the first authentic Chinese ovens in this country, his original restaurant, Hinky Dink's, which opened in 1934 in Oakland, California, attracted sophisticated San Franciscans in droves. The name was changed to Trader Vic's in 1936 and that same year Herb Caen, a Pulitzer Prize–winning columnist for the *San Francisco Chronicle*, wrote that the "best restaurant in San Francisco is in Oakland." The place was heavy on atmosphere, the original tiki bar. Vic himself said that the Pacific theme "intrigues everyone. You think of beaches and moonlight and pretty girls. It is complete escape."

Serves 4

¼ cup pineapple-apricot jam, or pineapple or apricot jam, preserves, or a combination

½ cup rum, preferably dark Jamaican

4 large scoops best-quality coconut ice cream (vanilla can be substituted)

8 rings very ripe, fresh pineapple, peeled and cored

2 ripe bananas, peeled and cut into thin rounds

½ cup shredded fresh coconut (or sweetened shredded coconut)

1. Place the jam and rum in a small saucepan and heat until warm.

2. Meanwhile, place an ice cream scoop in each of 4 large glass or other attractive bowls.

3. Cut the pineapple rings in half and arrange the halves around the base of the ice cream.

4. Arrange the banana slices over the pineapple and sprinkle with the shredded coconut.

5. Ignite the warm jam-rum sauce, stirring until the flames die out. Be careful not to catch anything on fire. Pour over the ice cream. Serve immediately.

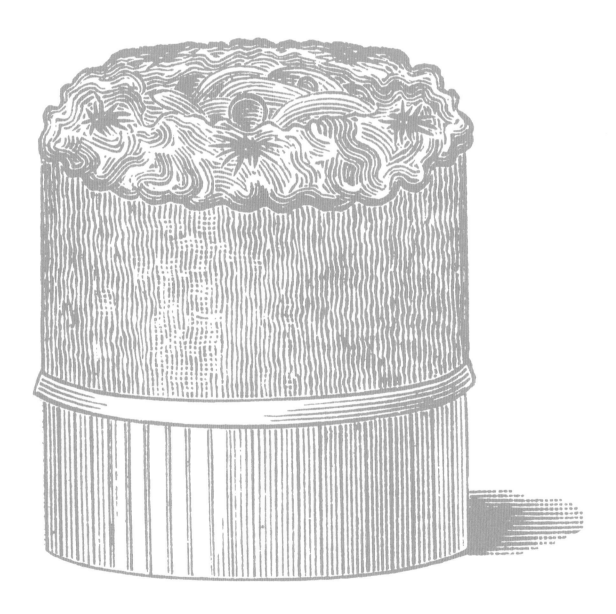

PANCAKES, CUSTARDS, and SOUFFLÉS

Antonin Carême's Soufflé Rothschild

New Orleans's Calas

Cannelés Bordelais

Josephine Baker Flan

Caramelized Plum and Raisin Clafoutis

The Zodiac Room's Caramel Soufflé with Custard Sauce

Henri Charpentier's Crêpes Suzette

Marcel Boulestin's Crêpes Verlaine

George Lang's Friars' Ears

Reuben's Apple Pancake

Forum of the Twelve Caesars's Mad Nero Crêpes

The Four Seasons's Coffee Cup Soufflés

ANTONIN CARÊME'S

Soufflé Rothschild

Antonin Carême's invention of the classic soufflé in the early 1820s was made possible by new ovens, which were heated by air drafts instead of by coal. This new technology provided the more even cooking temperature needed for a soufflé to rise properly and stay risen. Initially, Carême made his soufflés in stiff pastry casings that were not eaten. Their straight sides were the inspiration for our current soufflé dishes. He went on to create hundreds of other soufflés including the Soufflé Rothschild, which originally contained real gold and was aptly named by its creator in honor of his employer, at the time the richest man in France. It consisted of a pastry-cream base lightened with beaten egg whites and flavored with chopped crystallized fruits macerated in Danziger Goldwasser, a liquor containing suspended gold crystals. More modern recipes often substitute Kirsch or Cognac.

In the 1950s, the dessert was served as the pièce de résistance in fancy restaurants such as Manhattan's La Caravelle. Classically, the soufflé was surrounded with fresh strawberries, though there were exceptions. The Whitehall Club in Chicago doused it with zabaglione sauce (I've adapted their sauce recipe from *The Vincent Price Cookbook*.) Michel Roux's delicious variation contains honey and crushed macaroons in addition to the traditional candied fruit. Roux bakes his soufflés in individual ramekins and serves them topped with honey ice cream. Unadorned is also fine, although a dollop of whipped cream or half-melted vanilla ice cream is always welcome.

Serves 6

⅔ cup finely chopped mixed candied fruit (use at least three of the following: orange, citron, lemon, angelica, peach, pineapple, or cherries)

¼ cup Danziger Goldwasser, Kirsch, brandy, or Cognac

⅔ cup plus ¼ cup milk

¼ cup granulated sugar

2 tablespoons all-purpose flour

4 large eggs, separated, plus 2 egg whites, at room temperature

1 tablespoon unsalted butter, cut into little pieces

¼ teaspoon vanilla extract

Pinch of salt

¼ teaspoon cream of tartar

Confectioners' sugar

Large strawberries or raspberries (optional)

Whitehall Club Zabaglione Sauce (recipe follows) or crème anglaise (see recipe, page 190), whipped cream, or softened vanilla ice cream (optional)

1. Macerate the candied fruit in the liquor for at least 1 hour and up to several weeks.

2. Preheat the oven to 400 degrees. Butter and sugar a 6-cup soufflé dish or charlotte mold.

3. In a small saucepan, heat ⅔ cup milk with the granulated sugar and stir until the sugar is dissolved. In a small bowl, mix the flour with the remaining ¼ cup milk. Whisk the flour paste into the hot milk and bring to a boil, stirring until the mixture thickens. Lower the heat and simmer for 2 minutes, continuing to stir. Remove from the heat, then whisk in the 4 egg yolks, one at a time, and dot the top with butter pieces to prevent a skin from forming. When cool, stir in the fruit/liquor mixture and then the vanilla. (Covered, this soufflé base can be stored for up to 24 hours in the refrigerator. Heat to lukewarm before continuing, then stir to evenly distribute the fruit.)

4. Using an electric mixer fitted with the whisk attachment, beat the 6 egg whites together with the salt and the cream of tartar until stiff but not dry. Lighten the soufflé base with ¼ of the beaten whites and then fold the rest of the whites into the lightened base until just combined. Spoon into the prepared mold and bake in the middle of the oven for about 18 minutes or until the soufflé is well risen and golden. The center of the soufflé should remain a bit creamy (this is a matter of personal preference so cook longer if you like).

5. Sift confectioners' sugar over the top and serve the soufflé immediately, by itself or garnished with fresh berries and Whitehall Club Zabligone Sauce, crème anglaise, whipped cream, or softened vanilla ice cream.

WHITEHALL CLUB ZABAGLIONE SAUCE

Makes 3 cups (serves 6 to 8)

The Whitehall Club used a mixture of sherry and Grand Marnier, which enhanced the flavors of the dried fruits. You can substitute the liquor used in the soufflé.

3 large egg yolks
3 tablespoons sugar
2 tablespoons sherry (or the same liquor used in the soufflé)
Pinch of salt
⅛ teaspoon vanilla extract
½ cup cold heavy cream, whipped until soft peaks form
2 tablespoons Grand Marnier (or the same liquor used in the soufflé)

1. Place the first 5 ingredients in the top of a double boiler or in a medium-sized stainless steel bowl. Whisk vigorously until pale yellow.

2. Set over barely simmering water and cook the mixture, whisking constantly using a wire whisk, a hand-held electric mixer, or a rotary beater, until it is very thick, 6 to 10 minutes. Bring almost to a boil but do not actually boil or the mixture will curdle.

3. Remove from the heat and transfer to a clean bowl to cool.

4. When completely cool, fold in the whipped cream and the liquor of your choice.

New Orleans's Calas

On the streets of New Orleans's French Quarter, until the early 1900s, one could still find old black women, their hair wrapped in colorful bandanas, selling Calas. Folded into napkins to stay warm, the Calas were placed in wooden bowls that the women balanced on their heads while calling out "Belle cala! Tout chaud!" as they made their early-morning rounds.

Calas were originally made at home, first by slaves and then by housekeepers and cooks, and were sometimes eaten for breakfast as well as for dessert. As slave labor and then cheap black labor died out, so did this special fritter. They are a Creole dessert generally thought to have African roots, though in the book *The Carolina Rice Kitchen* (1992), Karen Hess argues convincingly that their roots were actually French, descending from French rice croquettes or "beignets de riz." She acknowledges, however, that the name itself comes from the West African word for fritters, "akkra," which was used by the slaves who initially made them.

Essentially sweet rice fritters, Calas are perfumed with nutmeg, deep-fried, and eaten very hot sprinkled with powdered sugar. Just-made Calas, with their crispy outsides and tender interiors (what Brillat-Savarin called "la surprise" when describing correctly made fritters), like popular French Quarter beignets, make a perfect breakfast, afternoon snack, or dessert. New Orleans–style chicory-flavored café au lait is the best accompaniment.

Serves 6 (makes about 18 Calas)

1 cup long-grain white rice
¾ teaspoon salt
1 package (¼ ounce) active dry yeast, dissolved in
    ¼ cup warm water
5 large eggs well-beaten, at room temperature
¼ cup granulated sugar
1 teaspoon freshly grated nutmeg
½ cup all-purpose flour
Tasteless vegetable oil for deep-frying, enough to fill a
    saucepan or deep fryer to at least 3 inches
Confectioners' sugar, for dipping or dusting

1. Put the rice, salt, and 4 cups water in a medium-sized saucepan over high heat. Bring to a boil, then reduce the heat and simmer until the rice is mushy and falling apart, about 25 minutes. If it becomes too dry, add a little water near the end.

2. Let the rice cool. When cool, pulse it in a food processor briefly to break up the rice, then transfer the mixture to a bowl, stir in the dissolved yeast, cover with a damp tea towel, and let it sit at least 8 hours or overnight.

3. Stir in the eggs, followed by the granulated sugar, nutmeg, and flour. Stir just to combine, then let the batter rest for 15 minutes.

4. Preheat the oven to its lowest setting and line a baking sheet with several thicknesses of brown paper or paper towels.

5. Put at least 3 inches of oil in a saucepan or deep-fryer. The oil should come no farther than one-third up the pan to prevent bubbling over when cooking. Heat the fat to 375 degrees on a thermometer. If using a fryer with a fry basket, put the basket in the oil to preheat. Be careful while frying. The oil is very hot and flammable. Do not let it slosh around or catch fire.

6. Carefully slip large spoonfuls of the batter (about 3 tablespoons each) into the hot oil. Depending on the size of your pan, fry 3 to 6 pieces at a time. It is important that you do not crowd the Calas. Leave them undisturbed until the bottom of each is golden brown, 1 to 2 minutes; when the bottoms are golden brown, use tongs or a slotted spoon to turn them. They are delicate, so be gentle. Cook until browned on the second side, another minute or two.

7. Use the tongs or a slotted spoon to transfer the fried batter to the prepared baking sheet. Pat them with more paper towels and place the pan in the oven. Repeat the process with the rest of the batter.

8. Place all of the Calas on a warmed platter and serve on warmed plates. Pass a bowl of confectioners' sugar for dipping the Calas, or sprinkle them with the sugar before serving. (I find that people enjoy dipping their own.) Though less traditional, Calas are also good with maple syrup or jam on the side (instead of the sugar).

Cannelés Bordelais

One day my good friend Lora Zarubin, food editor at *House and Garden*, intrigued me with her description of *cannelés bordelais*. She said cannelés were delicious but required expensive, hard-to-find fluted copper molds. A few days later I had dinner with Paloma Picasso and her husband, Eric Thevenet. When asked if they had heard of the dessert, they waxed on enthusiastically and told me that the scrumptious little cakes originated in the convent of Annonciades in Bordeaux in the 1700s and take their name from the molds, *cannelé* meaning "fluted" in French.

My curiosity piqued, the next day I plowed through cookbook after cookbook but found no mention of the mysterious cannelés. I eventually struck gold with French pastry chef Gaston Lenôtre and soon found additional recipes on French culinary websites. I located the copper molds at a specialty kitchen store and, despite the price, bought a dozen. Molds in hand, I went home and tried five different recipes. The version here is a combination of the three best.

Imagine a very rich little cake, soft and tender in the center, enveloped in a thick sugar-crisp fluted crust—a bit like a sweet and caramelized miniature Yorkshire pudding—perfumed with both rum and vanilla. This is a cannelé, and it can be eaten for any occasion. Pop one into your mouth like a doughnut for breakfast—they're perfect with a cup of coffee or tea—or serve for dessert accompanied by crème anglaise, berry sauce, or fresh fruit compote.

I work in batches with my twelve cannelé molds. You can do the same with however many molds you have. You can also halve the recipe.

Copper cannelé molds
1 quart plus 6 tablespoons whole milk
4 tablespoons (½ stick) unsalted butter
1 vanilla bean, split and scraped
4 large eggs, plus 4 large egg yolks
2½ cups sugar
1⅓ cups all-purpose flour, sifted
½ cup dark rum
Finely grated zest of 1 orange (optional)
Softened butter to grease the molds
Confectioners' sugar, for dusting (optional)

1. Heat the milk, butter, and the scraped vanilla bean and its seeds in a medium-sized saucepan until the mixture comes to a simmer. Turn off the heat, cover, and set aside.

2. Beat the eggs and egg yolks together with the sugar until light and fluffy, about 5 minutes using an electric mixer. Add the flour, rum, and orange zest (if using), and mix well.

3. When the milk mixture has cooled to lukewarm, strain it into the egg mixture and beat well. (Reserve the vanilla bean pods for another use.) Let the mixture rest at room temperature for 2 hours, then cover and refrigerate the batter for at least 24 hours and up to 72. The batter can be frozen for up to three months. Thaw before using.

4. When ready to bake the cannelés, preheat the oven to 400 degrees. Place the ½-cup cannelé molds on a baking sheet. Using a pastry brush, coat the insides of the molds very heavily with softened butter.

5. Fill the molds seven-eighths full and bake in the middle of the oven until the edges of the pastry are very dark brown, almost overcooked or a bit burnt in appearance. This will probably take at least an hour. It is difficult to tell when the cannelés are actually done. I find it is best to sacrifice one by cutting into it. Cannelés should be moist but not wet on the inside. If the trial cannelé is still wet when you cut into it, put the remaining cannelés back in the oven for 10 to 20 minutes. When a test proves them done, remove the cannelés from the oven and let cool for 15 minutes, then unmold them onto a wire rack.

6. Serve warm or at room temperature, plain or dusted with confectioners' sugar.

Josephine Baker Flan

On October 2, 1925, at the *Theatre de Champs-Élysées* in Paris, an unknown American dancer appeared on stage stark naked except for a hot pink flamingo feather between her legs. In a typical all-black "darkies on the bayou" number she jumped, gyrated, shimmied, and "dry-humped and slithered around her male partner and collapsed in a torrential orgasmic spasm" (as Betsy Prioleau wrote in *Seductress*, 2003). Josephine Baker brought down the house and by morning she had taken Paris by storm. Almost fifty years later, Janet Flanner wrote in her book *Paris Was Yesterday, 1925–1939*, "within half an hour of the final curtain on opening night, the news and meaning of her arrival had spread by the grapevine up to the cafes on the Champs-Élysées, where the witnesses of her triumph sat over their drinks excitedly repeating their report of what they had just seen." Baker was the poster girl of the 1920s: Calder sculpted her; Picasso painted her; women bobbed their hair à la Josephine; her name was on every lip. When she died in 1975 she was the first American woman to be buried in Paris with military honors. Twenty thousand people thronged the streets for her funeral procession.

A plethora of desserts were created and named after Baker on both sides of the Atlantic. Virtually all of them contained bananas, reflecting her time at the Folies Bergère, where she performed her outrageous and now legendary topless fertility dance wearing nothing but a skirt made from that very phallic fruit. The Josephine Baker Flan recipe below is adapted from Savarin's *Real French Cooking* (1956). His recipe uses only bananas. I have added pineapple and caramelize both fruits to intensify the flavor. Savarin included Kirsch and Chartreuse in his recipe. Combined with the flavor of the banana, this seems too tutti-fruttiesque; use rum instead. The sweetness of the rum-caramelized fruit is perfect with the eggy custard.

If you can, make this dessert ahead and refrigerate it overnight. The flavors will marry and further intensify. For a more elaborate presentation, caramelize the baking dish (as for the Caramelized Rice Pudding with Ginger on page 42) and unmold to serve.

Serves 6 to 8

3¼ cups milk
Finely grated zest of 1 lemon
1 cup sugar
4 tablespoons (½ stick) unsalted butter
½ small ripe pineapple, cut in half vertically, cored and
    very thinly sliced
2 small ripe bananas, thinly sliced
5 large eggs, plus 4 large egg yolks, at room temperature
½ teaspoon vanilla extract
2 tablespoons dark rum (such as Myers's)

1. Preheat the oven to 350 degrees.
2. In a small saucepan, bring the milk, lemon zest, and ¾ cup of sugar to a boil. Remove from the heat, stir, and set it aside to steep.
3. In a medium-sized skillet, melt the butter with the remaining ¼ cup sugar, stirring, over medium heat. Add the pineapple slices and cook until caramelized, stirring

occasionally. Stir in the banana slices and cook for 1 minute. Spread the fruit mixture evenly over the bottom of an 8-cup baking dish about 3½ inches deep.

4. Beat the eggs and egg yolks until well combined. Bring the milk mixture back to a simmer and gradually add it to the eggs in a thin stream, beating constantly. Stir in the vanilla and rum.
5. Strain the custard through a sieve over the fruit into the baking dish. Bake in a bain marie (a larger pan with hot water that comes halfway up the sides of the baking dish) in the lower third of the oven for about 40 minutes, until the custard is just set and a knife plunged into the center comes out clean. Do not overbake.
6. Serve warm, at room temperature, or chilled.

Caramelized Plum and Raisin Clafoutis

The Clafoutis is an ancient farmhouse dessert from Central France. The name comes from the provincial dialect word "clafir" (*clouter* in modern French), which can mean to nail down or stud and describes the effect of the cherries peeking through the batter. Wild black cherries are traditional (the pits were left in for flavor but this is risky business for teeth), but other fruits are sometimes used. The fruit is arranged over the bottom of an earthenware dish and then covered with a thick pancake batter sometimes laced with eau de vie.

There is some controversy regarding the best temperature at which to serve the dessert. Some recipes insist on serving it warm while others say temperature does not matter. George Sand, who spent a good deal of time in Berry, a major clafoutis city (although in the local dialect, it was called Galifouty) states categorically that it is neither good nor digestible served warm and is best when made in the morning for the evening or in the evening for the following day. However, I prefer my clafoutis warm, even if that means having to reheat it.

This recipe comes from close friends Babé and Pierre-Jean Pebeyre, truffle merchants who live in Cahors where they own and operate Pebeyre Ltd., started in 1897 by Pierre-Jean's great-grandfather. Like their business, this recipe has been in Pierre-Jean's family for generations. It deserves to be removed from its hiding place in Cahors and given international distribution along with their truffles.

As wild cherries are hard to come by, this Clafoutis uses plums and raisins instead. The Pebeyre's trick is to heavily caramelize the fruit before pouring the batter over. This makes a huge difference—the caramelization along with the Armagnac intensifies the flavor of the fruit and turns a simple farmhouse "pancake" into something sublime.

4 tablespoons (½ stick) unsalted butter

⅔ cup raisins, soaked in 3 tablespoons Armagnac until plump, at least 30 minutes

20 red plums, pitted and quartered, or 30 small black Italian plums, pitted and halved

6 tablespoons granulated sugar

3 tablespoons all-purpose flour

Pinch of salt

4 large eggs, plus 2 yolks

2 cups milk, heated and kept warm

1½ teaspoons vanilla extract

Confectioners' sugar, for dusting

1. Preheat the oven to 350 degrees.

2. Melt the butter in a 9- or 10-inch ovenproof skillet. (If you do not have an ovenproof skillet, after caramelizing the fruit, spread it evenly in the bottom of a 9- or 10-inch baking dish and continue with the recipe.)

3. Strain the raisins (reserve the Armagnac) and add to the pan along with the plums and 3 tablespoons of the sugar. Cook over medium heat until caramelized, about 5 to 10 minutes, stirring frequently. Set aside.

4. In a mixing bowl, combine the flour, salt, and the remaining 3 tablespoons sugar.

5. In a separate bowl, combine the eggs, egg yolks, and milk, and whisk to blend well.

6. Gradually stir the egg mixture into the flour mixture until well blended. Add the vanilla and the reserved Armagnac. Pour the batter through a sieve set over the fruit.

7. Bake for 40 minutes, or until set. Cool on a wire rack.

8. Serve (preferably) warm or at room temperature, dusted with confectioners' sugar.

Note: The dish can be made up to 1 day ahead and reheated for about 10 minutes in a 350-degree oven when ready to serve. Twenty apricots, five pears, or five apples can be used instead of the plums. If using apples, be sure to slice them thinly so they will cook through.

THE ZODIAC ROOM'S

Caramel Soufflé

WITH CUSTARD SAUCE

Helen Corbitt's legendary Caramel Soufflé is the type of dessert meant to be served from a trolley cart. It is a big, marvelous caramel meringue and paired here with a vanilla custard sauce (crème anglaise). Corbitt must have been influenced by the Portuguese molotov pudding, another caramel meringue and essentially the same dessert. To my taste, however, Corbitt's sauce is infinitely better than the overly sweet, eggy, yellow one that accompanies the pudding. A friend once told me that the purpose of Portuguese desserts is to use up the egg yolks left over when the nuns had used the whites to starch their habits. I have no idea if this is true, but if the molotov sauce is any indication, maybe it is. The Portuguese inclusion of toasted almonds adds visual appeal and is a crunchy contrast to the marshmallowy quality of the soufflé. I've added them along with a hard caramel drizzle to the original recipe given to me by Bertha Shields, who worked with Corbitt in the 1950s.

Two very similar classic desserts are *île flottante* and *oeufs à la neige*. Both, like Corbitt's soufflé, feature a soft meringue drizzled with hard caramel and floating on a crème anglaise. "Floating island," however, is a large baked meringue, while "eggs in snow" is composed of individual meringues that are poached rather than baked. These two desserts differ from the soufflé in that the basic meringue is flavored with vanilla rather than caramel.

Serves 6 to 8

About 3 tablespoons butter and ¼ cup sugar for
    preparing the cake pan
8 large egg whites, at room temperature
⅛ teaspoon salt
2 cups sugar, plus ½ cup for the hard caramel drizzle,
    if desired
½ teaspoon cream of tartar
1 teaspoon vanilla extract
2 teaspoons sifted cornstarch
Crème Anglaise (see recipe, page 190)
Raspberry Sauce (see recipe, page 190)
⅓ cup coarsely chopped toasted, blanched almonds
    (optional)

1. Preheat the oven to 425 degrees. Butter and sugar a 3-quart soufflé dish.

2. Using an electric mixer fitted with the whisk attachment, beat the egg whites together with the salt on low speed; gradually raise the speed to high and beat until stiff peaks form.

3. Meanwhile, place 2 cups of the sugar, the cream of tartar, and 1 cup water in a saucepan and bring to a boil, stirring until the sugar has dissolved. Cover and boil for 3 minutes. Uncover and continue to boil until the syrup is a dark caramel, and a candy thermometer reads approximately 375 degrees.

4. The egg whites should be ready by now. If they are ready before the caramel, turn off the mixer. The whites can wait a few minutes, but they must be ready before or at the same time as the caramel. So adjust stove heat and mixer speed accordingly. Or turn one or the other off for a bit if necessary. As soon as the caramel is ready, very slowly pour the caramel into the egg whites, beating constantly. Do this very slowly or the caramel may not incorporate properly.

5. Once all the caramel has been added, beat in the vanilla and the cornstarch.

6. Very gently spoon the mixture into the prepared soufflé dish; the soufflé mixture will rise above the top of the dish. This is okay as it will rise further when cooking and then sink as it cools.

7. Place the soufflé dish in a bain marie (a larger pan with boiling water to a depth of at least 2 inches). Put in the oven and immediately lower the oven temperature to 400 degrees. After 5 minutes, turn off the oven. Do not open the oven door. Let the soufflé bake for 15 minutes more, then remove it from the oven and place it on a wire rack to cool for 15 minutes. It will be golden and crusty on top.

8. Loosen the sides with a long knife and invert onto a serving plate.

9. If desired, make the hard caramel drizzle: Cook the ½ cup sugar with 3 tablespoons of water as described in step 3, until the caramel is dark. Pour it over the soufflé in a thin stream to make an interesting pattern on top. Let harden.

10. Serve cooled, accompanied by Crème Anglaise or Raspberry Sauce (even better with a tablespoon of Poire Williams added), or both, and sprinkled with the toasted almonds, if using. Or omit all sauce and simply garnish with fresh berries.

HENRI CHARPENTIER'S

Crépes Suzette

Henri Charpentier was born in Nice in 1890 and died in Redondo Beach in 1961. The intervening years had him working as a bellhop, head waiter, and finally master chef on the French Riviera before immigrating to New York in the early 1900s. There, in 1906, he opened the original Restaurant Henri's, which soon became world famous. From New York, Charpentier moved on to Los Angeles and opened another highly acclaimed Henri's, this time on Sunset Boulevard. His last stop was Redondo Beach where at his tiny and final restaurant, the sixteen-seat Henri Charpentier's, it was necessary to book a table four years in advance.

Among hundreds of others, famous guests at his restaurants included Queen Margherita of Italy, Sarah Bernhardt, "Diamond" Jim Brady, Theodore Roosevelt, William Jennings Bryant, and Ingrid Bergman.

In 1934, smack in the middle of his restaurant career, Charpentier wrote his book *Life a la Henri*. Alice Waters, in the introduction to the 2001 Modern Library Food edition wrote that these memoirs have the ". . . power to reveal the joys of living, and eating, with all your senses. Here is someone who never lost his almost infantile delight in life . . . a proud and happy sensualist whose memoirs span the turn of the twentieth century . . ."

It is in this book that Charpentier states his claim to having invented Crêpes Suzette. In 1894 he was fourteen and an assistant waiter at the Café de Paris in Monte Carlo. One day he served a party of seven men, including the Prince of Wales, and Suzette, the little daughter of one of the men. Although Charpentier was in the habit of making "French pancakes" virtually every day, somehow this time the cordials went up in flames. The prince was waiting; there was no time to start over. Charpentier tasted the sauce: to his surprise it was glorious. He realized that flame was exactly what had been needed to marry the ingredients. On the spot, he named his crêpes after the prince, who protested that there was a lady present and the crêpes should be named for her. The little girl rose, gave the prince a curtsy, and there you have it.

Crêpes Suzette are traditionally served with an intensely flavored citrus sauce, combining melted butter, orange or tangerine juice and zest, lemon juice, and sugar. The crêpes are then flamed tableside with Grand Marnier and Cognac. Many chefs beside Charpentier boast the creation of this classic, the legendary Auguste Escoffier being one of them. While Charpentier opts for half lemon and half orange juices, Escoffier's version insists on tangerine. Meanwhile *Larousse Gastronomique* quotes Leon Daudet's *Paris Vecu* (1920), which speaks of a specialty of Marie's in Paris, a pancake named Suzette made with jam and brandy. There is no mention of oranges, tangerines, or lemons, let alone the Prince of Wales or a little girl.

In *The Best of Boulestin*, Marcel Boulestin presents the theory that the dish was created in Paris by Monsieur Joseph at Restaurant Paillard during the 1890 World's Fair Exhibition and gives a decent argument to back this up. He goes on to give his own recipe—for Boulestin, the secret behind the intense flavor was rubbing sugar cubes against the skin of oranges before adding them, along with fresh orange juice, to the melted butter—while pointing out that the original recipe (whatever it was) has been much amended over time. He admits that perhaps Crêpes Suzette "like Homer's poems, are the production of several. Who can really decide its origin, name the inventor? And since we are dealing with a pancake, we might toss for it."

Serves 8

Makes 8 to 10 large crêpes

Make this batter at least 2 hours ahead and refrigerate before using. The batter can be made up to 3 days in advance and refrigerated or frozen for up to two months.

1¼ cups sifted flour
¼ cup plus 2 teaspoons superfine sugar
Pinch of salt
¼ teaspoon vanilla extract
1 whole egg plus 1 egg yolk
1¼ cups whole milk
1 tablespoon Cognac
1 tablespoon melted butter

1. Put all ingredients except the melted butter in a blender and blend on high until completely smooth and combined, about one minute.
2. Add the melted butter and blend for 15 seconds more. The batter should be slightly thicker than heavy cream. If too thick, thin with a little more milk.
3. Refrigerate for at least 2 hours and up to 3 days before using.

To make the crêpes:
1. Heat a 10- to 12-inch nonstick skillet over medium-high heat. Pour a quarter cup of batter into the pan. Immediately tilt the pan all around to coat the entire bottom and pour the excess back into the measuring cup.
2. When the crêpe is beginning to brown on the bottom, use a spatula to turn it over and brown the other side. Continue in this manner, layering the cooked crêpes in between sheets of wax paper when cool. You can make the crêpes ahead and store refrigerated or frozen until ready to use. Separate the crêpes from one another by placing a piece of wax paper between each.

To flame:
½ cup Cognac or brandy
1 cup orange liqueur such as Grand Marnier, Cointreau, Triple Sec, or curaçao
12 tablespoons unsalted butter (1½ sticks)
½ cup sugar, superfine is preferable
1½ cups fresh orange juice
2 tablespoons finely grated orange zest
1 teaspoon orange oil (optional)
8 large crêpes

1. Put the Cognac and orange liqueur in a small saucepan and set aside.
2. Melt the butter in a 16-inch (or larger) skillet over medium heat. Stir in the sugar, then the orange juice and zest, and the optional orange oil. When the sauce is hot and the sugar has dissolved, dip each crêpe in the sauce, put on a plate, and fold into quarters. Place the folded crêpes back in the pan. Use a spatula to turn them several times in the pan.
3. When the crêpes are heated through, warm the Cognac mixture and add it to the crêpes. Ignite the sauce to flame the crêpes, shaking the pan vigorously until the flames die out. Be careful not to catch anything on fire. Place each crêpe on a dessert plate and pour some sauce over. Serve immediately.

Crêpes Verlaine

Xavier Marcel Boulestin was born in Poitiers, France, in 1878, and spent his first eighteen years there. According to Maurice Firusk in the introduction to *The Best of Boulestin*, he lived "in the most attractive provincial manner, with a lively aesthetic sensitivity not only to the arts but in his daily observations of life and nature. [He was to] eventually devote his best years and efforts to the education of the English in French cuisine."

As a child Boulestin particularly loved music, food, and the garden; as a teenager he was an avid reader and soon became an avid writer. He was a journalist penning a weekly column on music for a Bordeaux newspaper before turning to fiction. While working on a short novel about a gigolo, called *Les Frequentations de Maurice,* Boulestin took frequent trips to Paris. His talent was soon spotted by Monsieur Willy (of Colette fame), who hired him as secretary and collaborator. Before long, the malicious gossip, scandal, and drama of la vie à la Willy became too much for him. Already a serious Anglophile, he crossed the channel and set up life in England en route to becoming "the most subtle, imaginative, and liberating food writer of his day," as Artemis Cooper puts it in *Writing at the Kitchen Table* (1999), her biography of the preeminent British cookery writer Elizabeth David.

Boulestin's early life in London was a bit of this, a bit of that. He dabbled in picture dealing and had a decorating business that went under after the war. He taught French, wrote a few articles, imported specialty French food products, and cooked in private homes for people who often asked for written recipes. At a particularly impoverished moment, he found himself at the publishing house of Heinemann, and asked offhandedly if a cookery book might interest them. The answer was yes, and a contract was signed on the spot. *Simple French Cooking for English Homes* was published in 1923 and reprinted several times. Boulestin also wrote cookery articles for many publications, including *Vogue, The Manchester Guardian,* and *The Daily Spectator.* In 1925, the same year his London restaurant Boulestin opened, *A Second Helping* was published, soon followed by *The Conduct of the Kitchen.* There were more books and articles. Boulestin was the first to teach the English, in straightforward and unpretentious language, how to prepare fresh, simple, and elegant French dishes and combine them to make easy, harmonious menus. His restaurant gave life to his food and menus. Elizabeth David praises his "intelligence, sense of taste . . . ease of style, un-scolding, un-pompous, un-sarcastic, ineffusive and to so high a degree inspiriting and creative."

Crêpes Verlaine caught my eye as I reread Elizabeth David's classic *An Omelette and a Glass of Wine.* There was a mystery and romance to the words written in barely legible script at the bottom of a charming illustration of a Boulestin Restaurant menu from September 26, 1936. Flipping through indexes of one Boulestin book after another, I eventually found the crêpes recipe in *The Finer Cooking* (1937), and then repeated in *The Best of Boulestin* (1952).

After describing the uncertain origins of Crêpes Suzette (page 176), Boulestin goes on to "stake my claim, so to speak, about Crêpes Verlaine. These are flavored with several liqueurs, and the final touch is given by absinthe. I chose the name for some fairly obvious and rather literary reasons. Verlaine, one of our great poets, was always fond of absinthe and at one time a schoolmaster in England and obviously a frequenter of Leicester Square. In one of the few poems he wrote during that time, he described how:

Le brouillard de Paris est fade

On dirait même qu'il est clair'

A côté de cette promenade

Que l'on appelle Leicester Square.

Mais le brouillarde de Londres est

Savoureux comme non pas d'autres."

[Parisian fog is bland / One could even call it transparent / Compared to this promenade / Which they call Leicester Square. / But London fog is savory like no other.] He created the dish in 1925 for his first restaurant, Boulestin, which opened that same year near Leicester Square.

Serves 8

8 large crêpes (see recipe, page 178)

½ cup Cognac or brandy

½ cup Kirsch

¼ cup Mandarine Napoléon (substitute an orange liqueur like Grand Marnier if you cannot find Mandarine)

¼ cup kümmel

2 tablespoons maraschino liqueur

¼ cup crème de cacao

2 teaspoons absinthe

12 tablespoons unsalted butter (1½ sticks)

½ cup plus 2 tablespoons superfine sugar

1 cup fresh orange juice

¼ cup fresh lemon juice

Finely grated zest of 1 lemon

1. Put the Cognac, Kirsch, Mandarine, kümmel, maraschino liqueur, crème de cacao, and absinthe in a medium saucepan and set aside.

2. Melt the butter in a 16-inch (or larger) skillet over medium heat. Stir in the sugar, the orange juice, lemon juice, and lemon zest. When the sauce is hot and the sugar has dissolved, dip each crêpe in the sauce, put on a plate, and fold it into quarters. Place the folded crêpes back in the pan. Use a spatula to turn them several times.

3. When the crêpes are heated through, warm the liqueurs and pour them into the pan over the crêpes. Ignite the sauce to flame the crêpes, shaking the pan vigorously until the flames die out. Be careful not to catch anything on fire. Place each crêpe on a dessert plate and pour the sauce over. Serve immediately.

Note: If you cannot find some of these liqueurs substitute curaçao, Triple Sec, or Grand Marnier for the Mandarine, Pernod for the kümmel, and omit the absinthe.

GEORGE LANG'S

Friars' Ears

(JAM-FILLED DERELYE)

A genius and man of many talents, Lang began his professional life as a violinist but at the age of twenty entered the world of gastronomy, where he has played a starring role ever since. *Fortune* magazine called him "the man who invents restaurants," and *The London Sunday Telegraph* called him a "world expert on culinary affairs." A brilliant restaurateur, Lang was a major player in Restaurant Associates, ran New York's famous Four Seasons restaurant in the 1960s, has owned and operated New York's Cafe des Artistes for many years, and even arranged a legendary state dinner in 1957 for Queen Elizabeth II. He is also the author of many articles and acclaimed books.

Now in his eighties, Lang is still working full throttle with the energy of an enthusiastic kid. He opened his vast cookbook library (one of the best in the country) to me when I was researching this book. That library and several conversations with him provided me with invaluable information. I am grateful for his intelligence, charm, humor, and generosity.

Friars' Ears is one of the simplest Hungarian noodle desserts, essentially nothing but jam dumplings served hot and garnished with white bread crumbs browned in butter and dusted with vanilla sugar. George Lang spoke nostalgically of his mother's homemade Friars' Ears—so named because they look like ears and because the friars ate them on Fridays when they were not allowed to eat meat. These dumplings were his favorite sweet as a boy. He encouraged me to include

this homey comfort food in this book not only because *derelye* are a delicious lost dessert, but also because hot noodles are "the Hungarian food preparation most different from that of other nations." Lang asserts that hot noodles are as crucial to the Hungarian cuisine as pasta is to the Italian. In Hungary, however, the noodle course is usually sweet and comes at the end of the meal.

In this adaptation of Lang's dish, I have added extra bread crumbs and changed the dough recipe slightly. The little triangular dumplings rise far above the few simple ingredients from which they are made. They're even better when sautéed in brown butter and served with heavy cream. Add a fresh fruit garnish to complement the jam—a few fresh raspberries sprinkled over if using raspberry jam, a sliced apricot and maybe a few berries for color with apricot jam, and so on. Try them for dessert, for breakfast, or for brunch, blintze-style.

Serves 4

2½ cups all-purpose flour
2 large eggs, at room temperature
2½ teaspoons salt
About ½ cup apricot jam, or jam flavor of your choice
½ cup (1 stick) unsalted butter
2 cups large bread crumbs made by crumbling good-
    quality white bread (not sourdough)
Vanilla sugar (see recipe, page 191)
Berries or diced fruit for garnish (optional)
1 cup heavy cream (optional)

1. Sift the flour into a large bowl and make a well in the center.
2. In a small bowl, whisk one of the whole eggs together with the yolk of the second (save the white to use later), ½ teaspoon of the salt, and ½ cup water, and pour the mixture into the well. Mix, then knead into a stiff dough. If the dough is too dry to hold together, add a bit more water. Knead until the dough is smooth and shiny. Form it into a ball and let it rest for at least 1 hour.
3. Sprinkle the work surface with flour, then stretch the dough and roll it to a ⅛-inch thickness or a bit thinner. If it becomes too elastic to roll, let it rest for 10 minutes or so before continuing.
4. For the most tender dumplings, let the dough rest once rolled for at least 1 hour and up to 24 hours before continuing. If you plan to wait longer than 1 hour, cover and refrigerate the dough.

5. Cut the rolled dough into 3-inch squares. Place a generous teaspoon of jam in the center of each square. Lightly beat the reserved egg white and use it to brush the edges of the squares. Fold each square into a triangle. Pinch the edges together and press with a fork or use a pie crimper to seal completely.
6. Bring at least 4 quarts of water to a boil in a large pot. Add the remaining 2 teaspoons salt and gently drop in the dumplings.
7. When the dumplings are done, after about 5 minutes, use a slotted spoon to place them in one layer on a tea towel. The dumplings can be prepared to this point a few hours ahead of time and covered with a damp towel. When ready to proceed, reheat the dumplings in boiling water or, even better, sauté them in butter before adding the bread crumbs.
8. Meanwhile, melt the butter in a large skillet and add the bread crumbs. Brown them, stirring constantly, and watching carefully so they do not burn. When they are golden brown, remove from the heat and add the warm dumplings to the skillet. Stir gently and turn so they are well coated in bread crumbs.
9. Transfer the dumplings to individual dessert plates or a serving platter. Sprinkle any crumbs that remain in the pan over the top and then sprinkle generously with vanilla sugar. Serve immediately, accompanied by berries and a pitcher of heavy cream, if desired.

REUBEN'S

Apple Pancake

Arnold Reuben bragged that his restaurant catapulted "from a sandwich into an institution." He invented his namesake sandwich when, in 1914, an actress filming with Charlie Chaplin supposedly requested the combination of grilled corned beef, Gruyère, Russian dressing, and sauerkraut on rye. The restaurant was certainly famous for "celebrity" sandwiches, which were named after the actors, actresses, dancers, and columnists who favored them. The list included Judy Garland, Walter Winchell, Jackie Gleason, Zsa Zsa Gabor, Dean Martin, and Frank Sinatra. In addition to sandwiches, both New Yorkers and tourists were also willing to wait in line for the famous cheesecake and this apple pancake.

Reuben's started in 1917 as a sandwich stand in Atlantic City. It then moved to New York—first to Broadway and Seventy-third Street and then to Madison Avenue. By the time the restaurant arrived at 6 East Fifty-eighth Street in 1928, Reuben had refined his winning formula and people flocked in droves to his walnut-paneled establishment with its red leather upholstery and gold-leaf ceiling. And there was still a sandwich counter by the entrance for those who wanted to get in and out quickly. As Michael and Ariane Batterberry write in *On the Town in New York*, "the mystique of Reuben's was that nothing ever changed—the stuffed-fish-and-sailboat non-décor was changeless, the grouchy waiters grew old but never died, the basic menu, its duckling and red cabbage, its apple pancake and its Reuben's chow mein remained unaltered."

For years, hungry theatergoers—and hungry actors—who craved simple deli food more than the fancier food and scene at Sardi's, hung out post-performance at Reuben's. Whenever I was in New York, whether attending theater or not, I joined the locals, went to Reuben's, and ordered the legendary apple pancake. The tender pancake, abundant caramel—often deliciously chewy and a bit burnt—and succulent apples always came together with spectacular results.

This twelve-inch pancake feeds four generously, but if you want something smaller and easier to flip, halve the recipe and use an eight- or nine-inch skillet. Though the raisins are optional—to be honest, I don't remember them in the original pancake—they are a delicious, highly recommended addition.

Serves 4 very generously (or 6 to 8 with accompanying cream, whipped cream, or vanilla ice cream)

1 cup all-purpose flour

¼ teaspoon salt

6 large eggs, at room temperature

1 cup milk, at room temperature

2 teaspoons vanilla extract

2 Granny Smith apples, peeled, cored, and sliced into
    ¼-inch wedges

¼ cup raisins (optional)

1 teaspoon ground cinnamon

1 cup sugar

12 tablespoons (1½ sticks) unsalted butter, cold

1 lemon, unsweetened whipped cream, vanilla ice cream,
    or a pitcher of heavy cream

1. Sift the flour together with the salt.

2. In a medium-sized mixing bowl, whisk the eggs together with the milk and vanilla extract. Slowly add the flour mixture and whisk until just smooth. Do not overmix. Set the batter aside.

3. In a small bowl, toss the apple slices with the raisins, if using, along with the cinnamon and ¼ cup of the sugar. Set aside.

4. In a 12-inch nonstick skillet over medium-high heat, melt 4 tablespoons of the butter. Cut the rest of the butter into 1-inch pats.

5. When the butter is melted and sizzling, stir in the raisin-apple mixture and cook, stirring often, until the apples have begun to soften, about 10 minutes. Turn the heat to high and cook, stirring constantly, until the apples are dark and caramelized.

6. Reduce the heat to medium-high and add a pat of butter to the pan. Stir until the butter melts, then pour the batter evenly over the apples to cover them completely.

7. Use a heatproof rubber spatula to pull the set edges of the pancake away from the sides of the pan (as when making an omelette). Continue to tilt the pan to allow the still-runny batter to seep under the set pancake and cook. Continue to do this until the pancake begins to firm up, 3 to 4 minutes.

8. Invert the pancake onto a serving plate. Melt another pat of the butter in the pan and sprinkle with 4 tablespoons of the sugar. Slide the pancake back into the pan, cooked side up, and cook until the underside is browned, 3 to 4 minutes. The pancake will become caramelized and sticky.

9. Repeat this process (inverting the pancake onto a serving plate, adding 1 pat of butter and 4 tablespoons sugar to the pan, returning the pancake to the pan, cooking until brown) two more times—once more on each side. It may be necessary to use a metal spatula to loosen the pancake from the plate.

10. At this point the pancake should be done; very dark and very caramelized, almost black in spots. If it is not done, cook on each side a bit more. The pancake should stay intact, but if somehow with all of the turning it does not, do not worry about it. Fit it back together as best as you can. It will taste exactly the same and it is so fabulous your guests will excuse you if it is less than gorgeous.

11. Divide the pancake into portions in the pan and use a spatula to transfer the portions to individual plates, serve from the pan at the table, or invert onto a serving plate.

12. Serve each portion with a wedge of lemon to squeeze over or pass a bowl of whipped cream, vanilla ice cream, or a pitcher of heavy cream.

Mad Nero Crêpes

Joe Baum claimed to have come up with the concept for the Forum of the Twelve Caesars restaurant while reading Apicius. He then purchased seventeenth-century Italian portraits of the Caesars from Julius through Domitian, and, accompanied by several other Restaurant Associates colleagues, went off to Italy. This was the first of many trips to search for ancient recipes, artifacts, statuary, and anything else they thought might appeal to a public raised on 1950s spectacle movies like *Quo Vadis, The Robe, The Ten Commandments,* and *Demetrius and the Gladiators.*

With its sixteen-foot ceilings, oversize silverware, huge brass service plates, waiters dressed in faux togas, and ice buckets made to look like the helmuts of centurions, the restaurant was flamboyant, ostentatious, over the top, and often tongue in cheek. The finest ingredients available were used in dishes with crazy names such as the flaming Fiddler Crab Lump à la Nero; Sirloin in Red Wine, Marrow, and Onions—a Gallic recipe Julius collected while there on business; and Mushrooms of the Sincere Claudius—an Emperor's Delight (it is thought that Claudius was intentionally poisoned by a mushroom). Campy as this may seem, the food was good enough for customers to take the restaurant seriously. They arrived en masse, clamoring to pay the restaurant's high prices. Within a few months of opening in 1958, Forum was *the* New York City destination restaurant.

I have adapted a recipe given to me by Tom Margittai, previous co-owner of the Four Seasons, another jewel in the Restaurant Associates crown. Typed long ago on three separate pieces of paper, it gives restaurant proportions starting with eight pounds nuts, twelve pounds butter, twelve pounds honey. The ingredients are very Roman—nuts, cinnamon, citrus, and honey (the Romans loved honey, even using it as a dip for garlic, radishes, and sauerkraut)—and the crêpes, with lots of flames and fire, are very Nero-esque.

Serves 8 to 10

For the filling:
1 cup (2 sticks) unsalted butter, at room temperature
1 ounce each roasted and finely chopped hazelnuts,
    blanched almonds, pistachios, pecans, and walnuts,
    a total of 1 cup of a combination of all five or of
    whatever you have (even two kinds of nuts produces
    a delicious result)
¾ cup honey
Large pinch of cinnamon (optional)
Juice and finely grated zest of ½ lemon

For the crêpe batter:
1¼ cups sifted all-purpose flour
5 scant tablespoons superfine sugar
Pinch of salt
¼ teaspoon vanilla extract
1 large whole egg, plus 1 yolk
1¼ cups whole milk, or more if needed
1 tablespoon Cognac
1 tablespoon unsalted butter, melted

For assembling the crêpes:
8 to 10 tablespoons each dark Jamaican rum, Cognac, and
    orange liqueur (Grand Marnier, Cointreau, Triple Sec,
    or curaçao) (3 tablespoons mixed liqueurs per crêpe)
8 to 10 tablespoons unsalted butter (1 tablespoon
    per crêpe)
8 to 10 teaspoons superfine sugar (1 teaspoon per crêpe)
1 to 1¼ cups fresh orange juice (2 tablespoons per crêpe)
8 to 10 teaspoons fresh lemon juice (1 teaspoon per crêpe)

To make the filling:
1. Using an electric mixer, cream the butter. Add the nuts.
Mix well, then add the honey and stir until well combined. Add the cinnamon, if using, and the lemon juice
and zest. Store filling, covered and refrigerated, for up to
several months.

To make the crêpes:
1. Put all the batter ingredients except the melted butter
in a blender and blend on high speed until completely
smooth and combined.
2. Add the melted butter and blend for 15 seconds more.
The batter should be slightly thicker than heavy cream. If

too thick, thin with a little more milk.
3. Refrigerate the batter for at least 2 hours and up to
3 days.
4. Heat a heavy nonstick 10- to 12-inch skillet over
medium-high heat. Pour ¼ cup of the batter into
the pan. Immediately tilt the pan all around to coat the
entire bottom of the pan and pour the excess back into
the measuring cup.
5. When the crêpe is beginning to brown on the bottom,
use a spatula to turn it over and lightly brown the other
side, then transfer to a plate. Continue making crêpes,
layering them between sheets of wax paper when cool.
You can refrigerate the crêpes, well-wrapped in foil for up
to 2 days, or freeze them for up to 2 months (defrost
before using).

To assemble the crêpes:
1. Spread 3 tablespoons of the filling on each crêpe.
Fold in half and then in half again. Set aside.
2. Combine the appropriate amount of liqueurs for the
number of crêpes you're making in a small saucepan
and set aside.
3. In a very large sauté pan (if you are preparing several
crêpes at a time) or in a 10- to 12-inch skillet (if you are
preparing one at a time), melt the appropriate amount of
butter for the number of crêpes you are making. Add the
approximate amount of sugar and then the orange and
lemon juices.
4. Stir the sauce and, when hot, place the folded crêpes
in the pan. Use a spatula to turn them several times.
When heated through, warm and ignite the liqueurs and
pour them over the crêpes, shaking the pan vigorously
until the flames die out. Be careful not to catch anything
on fire. Place each crêpe on a dessert plate and pour the
sauce over. Serve immediately.

Note: Margittai says the filling gets better with age, so
make a lot and keep it refrigerated until needed. In addition, the crêpe batter freezes well. You can also make the
crêpes themselves ahead of time. Separated with sheets
of wax paper and wrapped tightly, they will keep for at
least two days in the refrigerator and at least two months
in the freezer.

THE FOUR SEASONS'S

Coffee Cup Soufflés

Though these little soufflés were a very popular item on the menu at the Four Seasons from day one, the restaurant's longtime pastry chef, Patrick Lemble, recently decided to retire them. (He threw out the coffee cups as well!). They were always a favorite of mine. When the first *Four Seasons Cookbook* came out in 1971 containing the soufflé recipe, I could not wait to try it at home. Serving a coffee soufflé in a coffee cup is a bit of a gimmick, but one that I like. If you don't, use ramekins or small charlotte molds. The taste is the same. To this day, I find the partially thawed ice cream an ideal sauce for a variety of desserts; these soufflés are no exception.

Serves 8

7 tablespoons unsalted butter, at room temperature,
    plus more to grease the cups
7 tablespoons all-purpose flour
2¾ cups whole milk
3 tablespoons instant espresso powder such as Medaglia
    D'Oro
9 large eggs, separated, at room temperature
1 teaspoon cream of tartar
Large pinch of salt
1½ cups sugar, plus more to coat the coffee cups
2 cups coffee ice cream, softened

1. Preheat the oven to 425 degrees. Generously butter the insides of 8 ovenproof coffee mugs or individual 1-cup ramekins or charlotte molds and coat with sugar.
2. Cream the 7 tablespoons of butter together with the flour until completely blended.
3. In a medium-sized saucepan, bring the milk to a boil, then whisk in the flour-butter mixture, several tablespoons at a time, while continuing to cook. Once thick, remove from heat and cool to lukewarm.
4. Stir the instant espresso powder into the mixture, then stir in the egg yolks, one at a time. Spread plastic wrap directly on the surface to keep a skin from forming. The recipe can be made to this point up to 24 hours ahead and refrigerated. Remove the plastic wrap and put the pan over low heat and heat to just lukewarm before proceeding.

5. Using an electric mixer fitted with the whisk attachment, beat the egg whites together with the cream of tartar and salt, starting on low speed and slowly increasing the speed to medium, until soft peaks form. Add the 1½ cups sugar very gradually, while slowly increasing the speed of the mixer to high; beat until stiff but not dry.
6. Stir one quarter of the egg whites into the egg yolk mixture to lighten it, then fold the lightened mixture into the remaining egg whites until just combined.
7. Set aside 1 cup of the soufflé mixture.
8. Divide the remaining mixture among the prepared coffee mugs.
9. Bake until the soufflés are well risen and not too wobbly, about 12 to 15 minutes.
10. While the soufflés are in the oven, make the sauce by mixing the reserved soufflé batter with the ice cream.
11. When the soufflés are done, place them on individual plates and serve immediately. Pass the sauce separately.

Note: This recipe uses raw egg whites. If you are concerned about bacteria, or if serving to the young, elderly, or those with health issues, use pasteurized egg whites or liquid egg whites as a substitute. Also, there's less risk of bacteria with organic eggs.

Dessert Extras

RASPBERRY SAUCE

Makes approximately 1½ cups

1 (10- or 12-ounce) bag frozen raspberries or about
   2½ cups of fresh raspberries
½ cup sugar
Pinch of salt
Lemon juice to taste
1 tablespoon framboise, Poire Williams, or Kirsch
   (optional)

1. In a medium saucepan, cook the raspberries with the
sugar and salt over medium heat until they are broken
down completely and the sauce has thickened a bit,
5 to 10 minutes.
2. Strain the sauce through a sieve into a bowl, stirring
and pushing the fruit to obtain as much liquid as possible.
3. Add lemon juice to taste and once cool, the optional
liqueur. Store in a lidded container in the refrigerator. The
sauce will keep at least 3 weeks refrigerated.

CRÈME ANGLAISE OR VANILLA ICE CREAM BASE

Serves 8 to 10 (approximately 4½ cups)

2 cups milk
2 cups heavy cream
¾ cup sugar
Large pinch of salt
1 vanilla bean, split and scraped, or 1 teaspoon
   vanilla extract
8 egg yolks, at room temperature

1. In a medium saucepan, scald the milk and 1 cup of
the cream with the sugar, salt, and the seeds and pod
of the vanilla bean, if using.
2. Set aside to infuse for at least 15 minutes while you
prepare the rest of the recipe.
3. Using an electric mixer, beat the yolks until lightened
and thick.
4. Bring the hot milk mixture back to a simmer and add
it to the beaten yolks in a slow steady stream while beating constantly.
5. Return the mixture to the saucepan and cook over
medium low heat, stirring constantly, until thickened and
the mixture coats the back of the spoon. Do not let it
come to a simmer at this point.
6. Strain into a bowl. Add the remaining cup of cream
and cool. If you did not use the vanilla bean and seeds,
add the vanilla extract at this point. Refrigerate until
ready to use, up to 48 hours.

Note: This mixture makes delicious vanilla ice cream. To
make, cool and then refrigerate until cold before freezing
in an ice-cream maker according to manufacturer's
instructions.

SPUN SUGAR

2 cups sugar

1. Lightly butter aluminum foil or wax paper. Lightly butter a rolling pin.
2. Place the sugar and ⅔ cup water in a small saucepan and bring to a boil over medium heat, stirring constantly. Keep stirring until the mixture is completely clear.
3. Insert a candy thermometer in the liquid and continue to boil without stirring until the temperature reaches 310 degrees.
4. Remove the pan from the heat and let cool for 2 minutes until the caramel begins to thicken. This is very important. If the sugar is too hot or too cold (too thin or too thick) it will not form threads. Then place the pan of syrup in a larger pan of hot water to keep the syrup hot.
5. Hold the greased rolling pin in one hand and hold a wire whisk in the other. Dip the whisk in the syrup and quickly flick back and forth over the rolling pin. The sugar will run down and form long thin threads. Continue until the rolling pin is well covered with sugar threads.
6. Collect the threads and lay them on the greased foil or paper. They may be lightly flattened with a knife to make ribbons or gathered up to make a crown or other shapes.
7. Repeat until all the syrup is used up or until you have as many threads as you need. If the syrup gets too thick to use, reheat it.

Notes: Use the strands within an hour or two, otherwise they may melt, especially in humid weather.
This process can also be done between two greased rolling pins or broom handles balanced on stools or chairs.

VANILLA SUGAR

2 to 4 cups granulated sugar
1 vanilla bean, split in half vertically

1. Place the sugar in a jar or cannister with a tight-fitting lid.
2. Bury the vanilla bean in the sugar and seal tightly with the lid. Let sit for two weeks or longer. The sugar will keep indefinitely. When it is used up, just repeat the process with the same vanilla bean. It can be used repeatedly.

Note: You can also make vanilla sugar with the discarded pods used to make vanilla-steeped milk and cream for vanilla ice cream and crème anglaise. Just rinse them well in warm water, let them air dry for several days or dry in a low oven and then bury in the sugar. I save all of my discarded vanilla bean pods for this purpose.

Acknowledgments

Many people helped me with this book. First off, Dominique Browning, Lora Zarubin, and Betsy Pochoda gave life to the idea by publishing my "Lost Desserts" article in *House and Garden*; without them, there would have been no book. Next I would like to acknowledge the input, perseverance, good judgment, and sense of humor of my editor and friend, Ellen Nidy. Without her, I would have given up long ago. Thank you to Charles Miers for enthusiastically agreeing to publish *Lost Desserts*. And to my tireless agent, another good friend, Lisa Queen, who is always there when I need her. I greatly appreciate Barbara Kafka's making time to meet with me. In addition to sharing recipe suggestions, she put me in touch with George Lang and Tom Margittai who gave me books, recipes, and direction. Mr. Lang provided access to his extensive library, making me feel like a child in a candy store. I am grateful to both of them.

Thank you also to Nacht Waxman and Bonnie Slotnick. Their divine cookbook stores and personal treasure troves of information made the task of book writing easier and more fun. Michael and Ariane Batterberry, Nick Malgieri, and Mark Magowan also provided invaluable advice and guidance.

This book would have been an infinitely lesser entity without the tireless and brilliantly perfectionistic work of Eric Boman. I am extremely lucky to have him as a close friend and to have had him—with his genius, amazing eye, and depth of dessert knowledge (in addition to his knowledge of photography and design)—in charge of both the photography and the layout of my book. Thank you also to the spectacular book designers Miko McGinty and Rita Jules.

A very special thank you to Aunt Iva, who has been particularly supportive and helpful during this project (but more than that, during my entire life), and to my close friend, food mastermind Jeremiah Tower, who was always available to answer questions and to generously share his bottomless well of culinary information. Thanks to the super-tasters: my daughters Tess and Kate and many of their friends, David Nolan and his gallery staff, Ted Muehling and all the eaters in his perfect shop, Raul Barreneche, Daniel Cappello, Jane Edwards and her family, Peter Schlesinger, Mary and Walter Chatham, Edmund and Sylvia Morris, and all my cooking students— these people ate desserts as though there were no tomorrow.

The list of others to thank (for advice, consultation, support, and just general hand-holding) is long— please forgive any omissions. Certainly to be included are: Flavia Accolti-Gil; John Bare; Jo Bettoja; Alex von Bidder; Sara Blumberg; Diane Harris Brown; Beth Clements; Christine Donovan; Jerome Dreux; Brooke Hayward Duchin; Isabelle Collin Dufresne (Ultra Violet); John T. Edge; Meryl Evans; Anna Fogg; Jeffrey Hamelman; Virginia Hatley; Heidi Hough; Patrick Kinmonth; Albert Kumin; Michelle Laliatis; Patrick Lemble; Arthur Lubow; Nina Magowan; Susan Marcus; Theo and Ray Marcus; Marie Nugent-Head Marlas; Huguette Martell; Penny McPhee; Peter Meltzer; Babé and Pierre-Jean Pebeyre; Gerrie Pitt; Neil Ravenna; Carmen Robles; Emily Roos; Nora Slaff; Jim Slater; Lisa Slater; Roger Smith; Gabrielle Stelle; Liso Sterrit; Eve Stuart; Julia Thorne; Fabbio Trabocchi; Tessa Traeger; Cristina de Vogüé; and Joan Witkowski.

Acton, Eliza. *Modern Cookery for Private Families.* 1845. A facsimile of the first edition. East Sussex, England: Southover Press, 1993.

Adams, Charlotte. *The Four Seasons Cookbook.* New York: The Ridge Press, 1971.

Adams, Charlotte, and Doris T. McFerran. *The Family Cookbook: Dessert.* New York: Ridge Press, 1972.

Ali-Bab. *Gastronomie Pratique: Etudes Culinaires; Etudes Culinaires suivies du Traitement de l'Obésité des Gourmands.* Paris: Ernest Flammarion, 1928.

Batterberry, Michael, and Ariane Batterberry. *On the Town in New York: The Landmark History of Eating, Drinking, and Entertainments from the American Revolution to the Food Revolution.* New York: Routledge, 1999. First published, 1973 by Scribner's.

Beard, James. *Love and Kisses and a Halo of Truffles: Letters to Helen Evans Brown.* New York: Arcade Publishing, 1994.

Bergeron, Victor J. *Trader Vic's Book of Food and Drink.* Garden City, NY: Doubleday and Company, 1946.

——. *Trader Vic's Rum Cookery and Drinkery.* Garden City, NY: Doubleday and Company, 1974.

Black, René. *The René Black Cookbook: Cuisine Versus Cooking.* New York: Henry Holt and Company, 1955.

Boston Cooking School, The. *The Original Fanny Farmer 1896 Cook Book.* Baltimore, MD: Ottenheimer Publishers, 1996.

Boxer, Arabella. *A Second Slice: A Three-Tier Cookery Anthology.* London: Thomas Nelson & Sons, 1966.

Boxer, Arabella, and Jessica Gwynne. *Arabella Boxer's Book of English Food: The British Kitchen Between the Wars.* London: Hodder and Stoughton, 1991.

Boulestin, X. Marcel. *The Best of Boulestin: Choice Recipes of X. Marcel Boulestin; One of the World's Most Famous Chefs.* Surrey, England: The Windmill Press, 1952.

——. *The Finer Cooking; or, Dishes for Parties.* London: Cassell & Company, 1937.

——. *What Shall We Have Today?: 365 Recipes for all the Days of the Year.* London: William Heinemann, 1931.

Brillat-Savarin, Jean Anthelme. *Real French Cooking with a Selection of Outstanding Recipes from Other Countries.* Translated by E. M. Harr. Garden City, NY: Doubleday and Company, 1957.

The Brown Derby Cookbook, 50th Anniversary Edition. The Brown Derby International. Hollywood, California, 1976.

Bullock, Helen. *The Williamsburg Art of Cookery; or, Accomplished Gentlewoman's Companion.* 1938. A facsimile of the first edition. Williamsburg, VA: Colonial Williamsburg, 1966.

Cavallero, Gene, and Ted James. *The Colony Cookbook.* Indianapolis, IN: The Bobbs-Merrill Company, 1972.

Chamberlain, Samuel. *Clementine in the Kitchen.* New York: Hastings House, 1943.

Charpentier, Henri, and Boyden Sparkes. *Life a la Henri.* New York: Modern Library, 2001. First published 1934 by Simon and Schuster.

Child, Julia. *Mastering the Art of French Cooking: Volume One.* New York: Alfred A. Knopf, 1961.

Cooper, Artimis. *Writing at the Kitchen Table: The Authorized Biography of Elizabeth David.* New York: Ecco Press, 2000. First published 1999 by Penguin Group.

Corbitt, Helen. *Helen Corbitt's Cookbook.* Boston: Houghton Mifflin, 1957.

——. *Helen Corbitt's Greenhouse Cookbook.* Boston: Houghton Mifflin, 1979.

Cornetto, Anna Maria, and Jo Bettoja. *Italian Cooking in the Grand Tradition.* New York: The Dial Press, 1982.

Curnonsky. *Cuisine et Vins de France.* Paris: Librairie Larousse, 1987.

David, Elizabeth. *French Provincial Cooking.* London: Michael Joseph, 1960.

——. *Harvest of Cold Months.* London: Michael Joseph, 1999.

——. *An Omelette and a Glass of Wine.* London: Robert Hale, 1984.

Dennery, Linda, and Marcelle Bienvenu, eds. *The Picayune's Creole Cook Book.* Sesquicentennial Edition. New York: Random House, 1987.

Devonshire, Duchess of. *The Duchess of Devonshire's Chatsworth Cookery Book.* London: Francis Lincoln, 2003.

Ducasse, Alain. *Dictionnaire Amoureux de la Cuisine.* Paris: Editions Plon, 2003.

Escoffier, Auguste. *The Escoffier Cookbook.* New York: Crown Publishers, 1941.

——. *Ma Cuisine.* Translated by Vyvyan Holland. London: Hamlyn, 1965.

——. *Memories of My Life.* Translated by Laurence Escoffier. New York: Van Nostrand Reinhold, 1997.

de la Falaise, Maxime. *Seven Centuries of English Cooking.* New York: Grove Press, 1973.

Field, Michael. *Michael Field's Cooking School.* New York: Holt, Rinehart, and Winston 1965.

Flanner, Janet Genet. *Paris Was Yesterday: 1925–1939.* Rev. ed. Fort Washington, PA: Harvest Books, 1988.

Fowler, Damon Lee. *Classical Southern Cooking: A Celebration of the Cuisine of the Old South.* New York: Crown Publishers, 1995.

Garvin, Kevin, and John Harrisson. *Neiman Marcus Cookbook.* New York: Clarkson Potter, 2003.

Godard, Odile, and Maquelonne Toussaint-Samat. *Cuisine d'amour Méditerranée.* Arles, France: Actes Sud, 2000.

Goodwin, Betty. *Chasen's: Where Hollywood Dined; Recipes and Memories.* Santa Monica, CA: Angel City Press, 1996.

——. *Hollywood du Jour: Lost Recipes of Legendary Hollywood Haunts,* Santa Monica, CA: Angel City Press, 1993.

Grigson, Jane. *Good Things.* London: Penguin Books, 1973.

Guste, Roy F., Jr. *Antoine's Restaurant Since 1840 Cookbook: A Collection of the Original Recipes from New Orleans Oldest and Most Famous Restaurant.* New Orleans: Carbery-Guste, 1979.

Heath, Ambrose. *Good Food on the Aga.* Rev. ed. London: Persephone Books, 2003. First published 1933 by Faber and Faber.

Hess, Karen. *The Carolina Rice Kitchen: The African Connection.* 1901. A facsimile of the first edition. Columbia, SC: University of South Carolina Press, 1992.

Hill, A. P. *Mrs. Hill's New Cook Book: A Practical System for Private Families; in Town and Country.* Rev. ed. Bedford, MA: Applewood Press, no date. First published 1867 by Carlton Publisher Madison Square.

Hirsch, Sylvia Balser. *Miss Grimble Presents Delicious Desserts.* New York: Macmillan, 1983.

Jekyll, Agnes. *Kitchen Essays.* London: Persephone Books, 2001. First published 1922 by Thomas Nelson & Sons.

Kafka, Barbara. *The James Beard Celebration Cookbook.* New York: William Morrow & Co, 1990.

Kelly, Ian. *Cooking for Kings: The Life of Antonin Carême, the First Celebrity Chef.* London: Short Books, 2003.

Killeen, Jacqueline. *101 Secrets of California Chefs: Original Recipes from the State's Great Restaurants.* San Francisco: 101 Productions, 1969.

Klapthor, Margaret Brown. *The First Ladies Cook Book, Favorite Recipes of all the Presidents of the United States.* New York: Parents' Magazine Press, 1965.

Knopf, Mildred O. *The Perfect Hostess of Today.* New York: Alfred A. Knopf, 1950.

Lady Clark of Tillypronie. *The Cookery Book of Lady Clark of Tillypronie.* 1901. A facsimile of the first edition. East Sussex, England: Southover Press, 1994.

Lady Morgan. *France, In 1829–30.* New York: J&J Harper, 1830.

Lang, George. *The Café des Artistes Cook Book.* New York: Clarkson N. Potter, 1984.

——. *George Lang's Compendium of Culinary Nonsense and Trivia.* New York: Clarkson N. Potter, 1980.

——. *George Lang's Cuisine of Hungary.* New York: Atheneum, 1971.

——. *Nobody Knows the Truffles I've Seen.* New York: Knopf, 1998.

Lenôtre, Gaston. *Lenôtre's Ice Creams and Candies.* Translated by Philip and Mary Hyman. Woodbury, NY: Barron's Educational Series, 1979. Originally published as *Faites Vos Glaces et Votre Confiserie Comme Lenôtre* (Paris: Flammarion et Cie, 1978).

Leteuré, Marie. *Douceurs d'Antan.* Paris: Editions Solar, 2003.

Lewis, Edna. *The Taste of Country Cooking.* New York: Alfred A. Knopf, 1990.

——. *In Pursuit of Flavor.* New York: Alfred A. Knopf, 1988.

Liebling, A.J. *Between Meals: An Appetite for Paris.* 1959. A facsimile of the first edition. New York: North Point Press, 1986.

Lomonaco, Michael, and Donna Forsman. *The "21" Cookbook.* New York: Doubleday, 1995.

Malgieri, Nick. *How to Bake.* New York: HarperCollins, 1995.

Margittai, Tom, Paul Kovi, and Josef Renggli. *The Four Seasons: The Ultimate Book of Food, Wine and Elegant Dining.* New York: Simon and Schuster, 1980.

Mariani, John, and Alex von Bidder. *The Four Seasons: A History of America's Premier Restaurant.* New York: Crown Publishers, 1994.

Marie, Tante. *La Véritable Cuisine De Famille Par Tante Marie.* Edited by A. Taride. Paris: 1975.

Mauduit, Vicomte de. *The Vicomte in the Kitchen.* London: Robert Anscombe & Co., 1933.

Médecin, Jacques. *Cuisine Nicoise: Recipes from a Mediterranean Kitchen.* Harmondsworth, England: Penguin Books, 1983. Originally published as *La Cuisine du Comté de Nice* (Paris: Juilliard, 1972).

Montagné, Prosper. *Larousse Gastronomique: The World's Greatest Culinary Encyclopedia.* New York: Clarkson Potter, 2001.

Nignon Édouard. *Éloges* de la *Cuisine Française.* Paris: Francois Bourin, 1992.

O'Sullivan, Michael. *Le Coq Hardi, The Story of John Howard and His Restaurant.* Dublin: Blackwater Press, 2003.

Paddleford, Clementine. *How America Eats.* New York: Scribner's, 1960.

Paston-Williams, Sara. *The National Trust Book of Traditional Puddings.* London: David and Charles, 1983.

Pellaprat, Henri-Paul. *Modern Culinary Art: French and Foreign Cookery.* Paris: Jacques Kramer, 1950.

Pennell, Elizabeth Robins. *A Guide for the Greedy by a Greedy Woman.* 1922. A facsimile of the first edition. Kegan Paul: London, 2003.

Point, Fernand. *Ma Gastronomie.* Introduction and presentation by Felix Benoit. Wilton, CT: Lyceum Books, 1974.

de Pomiane, Eduard. *Cooking with Pomiane.* Random House, New York, 2001. First published 1976 by Faber and Faber.

Price, Mary and Vincent Price. *A Treasury of Great Recipes: Famous Specialties of the World's Foremost Restaurants Adapted for the American Kitchen.* New York: Ampersand Press, 1965.

Rawlings, Marjorie Kinnan. *Criss Cross Cookery.* New York: Scribner's, 1942.

Reisman, Rose, *Manhattan's Dessert Scene: New York City's Top Dessert Spots Reveal Their Secret Recipes.* Toronto: Lymas Publications, 1989.

Ridley, Helen. *The Ritz-Carlton Cook Book and Guide to Home Entertaining.* New York: J. B. Lippincott Company, 1968.

Ritz, Marie Louise. *César Ritz: Host to the World.* Philadelphia: J. B. Lippincott Company, 1938.

Rombauer, Irma, Marion Rombauer Becker, and Ethan Becker. *The All New, All Purpose Joy of Cooking.* Rev. ed. New York: Scribner, 1997. First published 1931 by Simon and Schuster.

Rosenzweig, Anne. *The Arcadia Seasonal Mural and Cookbook.* New York: Harry N. Abrams, 1986.

Roux, Michel. *Desserts: A Lifelong Passion.* London: Conran Octopus Limited, 1994.

Sax, Richard. *Classic Home Desserts.* Shelburne, VT: Chapters Publishing, 1994.

Scherer, Francine, and Madeline Poley. *The Soho Charcuterie Cookbook: Fabulous Food for Entertaining.* New York: William Morrow and Company, 1983.

Senderens, Alain. *The Table Beckons.* New York: Farrar, Straus, and Giroux, 1993.

Simmonds, Peter Lund. *The Curiosities of Food; or, the Dainties and Delicacies of Different Nations Obtained from the Animal Kingdom.* With an introduction by Alan Davidson. Berkeley: Ten Speed Press, 2001.

Simmons, Amelia. *The First American Cookbook: A Facsimile of "American Cookery."* 1796. Introductory essay by Mary Tolford Wilson. Mineola, NY: Dover Publications, 1984.

Smith, Delia. *Delia Smith's Christmas.* New Ed. London: BBC Books, 1994.

Soltner, Andre, and Seymour Britchky. *The Lutece Cookbook.* New York: Alfred A. Knopf, 1995.

Taylor, John Martin. *Hoppin' John's Low Country Cooking.* New York: Bantam Books, 1992.

Toklas, Alice B. *The Alice B. Toklas Cookbook.* New York: Harper and Row, 1954.

———. *Aromas and Flavors of Past and Present.* 1958. A facsimile of the first edition. New York: Lyons Press, 1996.

Toussaint-Samat, Maquelonne. *La Très Belle et Très Exquise Histoire des Gâteaux et des Friandises.* Paris: Flammarion, 2004.

Tower, Jeremiah. *Jeremiah Tower's New American Classics.* Scranton, NY: HarperCollins, 1986.

Veyrier, Henri. *Le Grand Dictionnaire de Cuisine d'Alexandre Dumas.* Madrid: Rivadeneyra, S. A., 1973.

Vickery, Phil. *Proof of the Pudding.* London: Simon and Schuster UK, 1999.

Wechsberg, Joseph. *Blue Trout and Black Truffles: The Peregrinations of an Epicure.* Chicago: Academy Chicago Publishers, 1985.

———. *Dining at the Pavillon.* Boston: Little, Brown, and Company, 1962.

White, Florence. *Good Things in England.* London: Persephone Books, 1999. First published 1932 by Jonathan Cape.

Willan, Anne. *Great Cooks and Their Recipes: from Taillevent to Escoffier.* London: Pavillion Books Limited, 1995.

Wolfert, Paula. *The Cooking of Southwest France: Recipes from France's Magnificent Rustic Cuisine.* New York: The Dial Press, 1983.

Index

First published in the United States of America in 2007

by Rizzoli International Publications, Inc.

300 Park Avenue South

New York, NY 10010

www.rizzoliusa.com

© 2007 Gail Monaghan

Photographs © 2007 Eric Boman

Art Director: Eric Boman

Designers: Miko McGinty and Rita Jules

2007 2008 2009 2010 / 10 9 8 7 6 5 4 3 2

Printed in China

ISBN-13: 978-0-8478-2983-5

Library of Congress Catalog Control Number: 2007930706